Ten Child-Centered Forensic Family Evaluation Tools

An Empirically Annotated User's Guide

Benjamin D. Garber, PhD
Psychologist

HIGH CONFLICT INSTITUTE PRESS
Scottsdale, Arizona
2015

Publisher's Note

This publication is designed to provide accurate and authoritative information about the subject matters covered. It is sold with the understanding that neither the author nor publisher are rendering legal, mental health, medical, or other professional services, either directly or indirectly. Neither the author nor the publisher shall be liable or responsible for any loss or damage allegedly arising as a consequence of your use or application of any information or suggestions in this book.

Cover design: Kristen Onesti

TO ORDER MORE COPIES: contact HCI Press at 1-888-986-4665, or www.hcipress.com.

Printed in the United States of America

Caveat Emptor

Your purchase of this volume constitutes license to copy and administer any one or more of the resources contained herein for professional purposes, including graduate level education. Your choice to use any one or more of these resources further constitutes acceptance of any associated liability.

These resources are not to be construed as psychometric tests. They have no established reliability or validity. They do not generate diagnoses. These are simply standardized protocols with which the family law professional can begin to collect, organize, compare and contrast data obtained from litigating caregivers. In particular, these resources have proven to be extremely valuable when they are front-loaded in an evaluation, that is, when prospective evaluation participants are asked to complete and return them in advance of first interviews. Used in this manner, these resources can assist the evaluator to streamline the evaluation process, to focus on particular areas of concern and to better understand and explore the areas in which caregivers agree and disagree. Front-loading these resources can also provide the evaluator with critical process-oriented information relevant to the manner in which participants organize, prioritize and meet deadlines more generally.

The reader is reminded that these resources, like so much relevant to mental health evaluation and family law process, are very language- and culture-dependent. The resources contained in this volume generally require respondents to have an eighth grade education, a mastery of English, and to have been enculturated in the contemporary United States. Administration and/or interpretation of these resources with individuals who do not meet these minimal criteria are likely to confound what is already a very complex and controversial process, namely, evaluation in the context of child-centered litigation.

Finally, and most obviously, data collected via administration of these resources, singly or in any combination, must not be mistaken as sufficient for any child-centered evaluation process. Under the best of circumstances, these resources can help to build a framework that the evaluator then fills in with data obtained via interview, observation and assessment so as to best understand the child and the family and thereby advise the court.

B.D. Garber, PhD
February, 2015

Table of Contents

The CD-ROM containing the downloadable/printable forms can be located inside the back cover.

You may also access the forms here:
http://wp.me/P51LWQ-bl OR

Introduction

On the development, administration, interpretation and integration of standardized questionnaire data

I am a forensic psychologist in private practice in New England. I came to this work, like so many family law professionals, very indirectly and unexpectedly.[1] My path began with interests in architecture and then linguistics, paused to consider how emotion and relationships impact the development of language and thought, and then took a sharp right turn when it struck me as impossible that eight out of every ten children referred to an outpatient psychology clinic had attention deficit hyperactivity disorder (ADHD).

Looking beyond a child's high energy and distractibility revealed what should have been obvious from the start: Living in the midst of chaos, confusion and conflict can interfere with any individual's ability to concentrate, control impulses and achieve in school. Some unknown but significant number of children who are diagnosed with ADHD, enlisted in associated treatments and/or administered stimulant medications are better understood as the victims of family stresses.[2] High conflict divorce. Separation from a parent or sibling. Relocation. Abuse and neglect. In short: the purview of family law.

As you may have discovered yourself, once a professional develops an interest in working with high conflict families, the floodgates open. In my experience, this is because many professionals are overwhelmed if not already scarred by the complexity and liabilities associated with these families.

Indeed, the evaluation and treatment of court-involved children can be daunting tasks. The professional is challenged to walk a tight rope between warring parties, to collect

---

[1] The final chapter of my "Developmental Psychology For family Law Professionals" summarizes the scant but fascinating literature on the professional development of lawyers and psychologists who chose to work in family law (Garber, 2009).

[2] To be clear: attention deficit (hyperactivity) disorder is a very real neurodevelopmental difference. There are excellent cognitive-behavioral and pharmacological treatments for ADHD. High conflict family dynamics and diagnosis of ADHD in one or more children are not mutually exclusive, but some children are mistaken as having ADHD when, in fact, they are responding to the chaos in their lives.

and interpret histories that are routinely disputed and pock-marked by the landmines that are restraining orders and arrests, allegations of violence and abuse, misunderstood and misused charges of alienation, estrangement and enmeshment. This same tight-rope-walking professional is alternately held aloft or weighted down by amorphous collections of ethical guidelines, standards of practice and jurisdictional mandates (e.g., AACAP, 1998; APA, 2010; AFCC, 2007; Herman, 1997). All this must be juggled while still atop the high wire with a knowledge of fields as diverse as child development, family dynamics, and the ever-growing literatures concerning domestic violence, substance addiction, and a long list of others.

Those who run away from the prospect of evaluating or treating families of this sort are probably wise. If you're reading this, however, you likely agree that working with these families to help the courts to better understand and serve the needs of children is the most challenging, thought-provoking and important work one can do.

I cope with the complexities and stresses of this work in part by organizing. Systematizing. There is so much that is unpredictable and uncontrollable when one is evaluating a high conflict family system, that it is critical to predict and control all that can be predicted and controlled. Thus, I began to develop standardized questionnaire and interview tools almost twenty years ago. This volume presents ten such tools.

A standardized questionnaire or interview is not an assessment instrument, per se. None of the resources contained in this volume have now or are likely to ever have established reliability or validity coefficients. None of these resources generate diagnoses.

Each of these resources is intended to provide you, the evaluating family law professional, with one among many perspectives on the matter at hand[3]; the means to draw a map to guide you through the complex family system. They provide grist for the mill and added value to the process. Each of these resources invites one or more of four specific applications:

First, I strongly prefer to front-load my evaluations with these resources. This means that upon receipt of an enabling court order, I deliver a Service Agreement (contract) detailing the proposed evaluation together with a sheaf of questionnaires, all of which must

---

[3] The Association of Family and Conciliation Courts (AFCC, 2007) and The American Psychological Association's (2010) child custody guidelines (among others) require that evaluators "… strive to employ multiple methods of data gathering" (item 10, p. 866).

be completed and returned before I will schedule initial interviews. I find that review of these completed materials in advance of interview helps to streamline the process, highlight hot spots, and determine what further instruments, interviews, observations and references I will seek. In this regard, I consider the time necessary to review the parties' completed questionnaires a significant savings as compared to the prospect of finding my way from the first interview forward with no such guide posts.[4]

Second, when two (or more) caregivers are each asked to complete the same standardized instruments, Parent A's responses can be contrasted with Parent B's responses so as to highlight their similarities and differences. In my experience using these resources with scores of families over many years, I never cease to be astonished by such differences. Parents can disagree on the "**Child Development Questionnaire**" regarding the date of their marriage, the date and conditions of their child's birth or their divorce. Mom might identify eight year old Suzy as calm and quiet and compliant on the "**Perceptions of My Child (and Summary Sheet)**" questionnaire while Dad describes the same child in completely opposite terms. Each of a pair of conflicted caregivers may credit him- or herself as willing and able to cooperate on the "**Co-parenting Questionnaire**" while blaming their parenting partner for stalemating the relationship.

Third, caregiver responses on these resources can provide critical reality checks when compared to third-party, first-hand and/or objective data. Thus, a parent's response on "**The Child's World**" questionnaire can be compared to the child's own professed favorite color or song or TV show. Another parent's responses on the "**Parenting Capacity Questionnaire**" or the associated semi-structured interview can be compared to direct observation of the parent and child interaction, the child's report and to third party report. Discovering that a parent can't name a child's best friends, doesn't know how the child is doing in school or the name of her medication must never in and of itself be reason to recommend against custody or for termination or become the basis for a schedule of parenting rights and responsibilities, but these clues, discovered up front, can guide further inquiry so as to gradually rule-in and rule-out these and similar recommendations.

Fourth, the way in which a caregiver responds to the prospect of completing a sheaf of questionnaires delivered at the start of an already anxiety-inducing court-ordered

---

[4] I note that Hynan (2014) makes a point of requesting that some such paperwork be completed in the office so as to minimize the possibility of taint. Birnbaum et al., (2008) recommend that if paperwork is completed off-site (or out of sight, perhaps) that the respondent be asked to assure that no one else contributed.

evaluation process is valuable data, regardless his or her actual responses. The task is not unlike what is required of parents routinely by their children's schools and pediatricians and mental health providers, not to mention the Internal Revenue Service, local bureaucracies and courts. Each of these tests the respondent's executive functions: The ability to organize, prioritize, and express a potentially overwhelming array of data. The parent who returns your sheaf of pre-evaluation questionnaires within days, color-coded, annotated and cross-referenced likely provides a very different caregiving environment than the parent who needs reminders, who returns questionnaires that are incomplete, stained and written in crayon. It is critical to understand that neither presentation is necessarily better or worse, simply that both the content- and process-differences between caregivers highlighted by these resources must be explored as they bear on the question at hand.

I have already provided the caveat about language and culture at the opening of this volume, but it bears repeating here: The resources provided here generally require that respondents have at least an eighth grade education and are comfortable with reading and writing in English. Interpretation of the data gleaned using these resources must take into account the respondent's culture and religion. To ignore these and related variables is to misuse these resources, to risk misunderstanding the respondent and to risk harming the child whose well-being is at issue (e.g., Klebanov & Travis, 2015).

How to use this volume: What follows is an introduction to each of ten evaluation tools presented in a sequence of six broad categories or chapters. Each chapter begins with an introduction to the general topic, including an annotated discussion of the resource. Each chapter closes with a brief list of references. The resources are laid out in between, page-by-page. I've included empirical citations intended to highlight aspects of each tool that I have found particularly interesting or valuable. When possible, I cross-reference items within a given resource with related data that is available elsewhere.

It is important to understand that the references, commentary and citations provided here are neither comprehensive nor necessarily even representative. I have provided the data that I believe may be a good starting point if and when a caregiver's response raises a red flag for you. The astute forensic evaluator will move from the red flag ("hmmm... I wonder what that means?") to elaboration in interview and/or cross-reference with objective records and then to the relevant literature. Keep in mind that the articles that I reference themselves have citations, and so on, so that a little effort may yield a fairly broad and current perspective on the issue. (see Gould & Martindale, 2008 regarding the importance of empirically sound evaluations).

This volume introduces and discusses ten tools, but it does not contain samples ready to duplicate for use. These are available to individuals who have purchased this volume **on the accompanying disk**. Your responsibility is to use the tools wisely, to respect the legal limitations of copyrighted materials, and to work conscientiously to serve the needs of court-involved children.

Good luck.

References

American Academy of Matrimonial Lawyers. (1997). *Practice parameters for child custody evaluation.* Available online from www.aacap.org.

American Psychological Association. (APA; 2010). Guidelines for child custody evaluations in family law proceedings. *American Psychologist*, 65, 863-867.

Association of Family and Conciliation Courts. (AFCC; 2007). Model standards of practice for child custody evaluation. *Family Court Review*, 45(1), 70-91.

Birnbaum, R.; Fidler, B.J. & Kavassalis, K. (2008). *Child Custody Assessments.* Ontario: Carswell.

Gould, J. W. Martindale, D. A. (2008). Custody evaluation reports: The case for references to the peer-reviewed professional literature. *Journal of Child Custody*, 5(3/4), 217-227.

Herman, S. P. 1997. Practice parameters for child custody evaluation: American Academy of Child and Adolescent Psychiatry. *Journal of the American Academy of Child and Adolescent Psychiatry* 36 (10): 578-688.

Hynan, D. (2014). *Child Custody Evaluations.* Charles C. Thomas: Springfield, Illinois.

Klebanov, Marianna S. & Travis, Adam D. (2015). *The critical role of parenting in human development.* New York, NY, US: Routledge/Taylor & Francis Group.

A. Third Party Personal References

Rationale and uses

The American Psychological Association's Guidelines for Child Custody Evaluation (2010; item 10) require, in relevant part that, "Psychologists strive to employ multiple methods of data gathering." This includes, "…access to documentation" from a variety of sources (e.g., schools, health care providers, child care providers, agencies and other institutions) and (…) members of the extended family, friends and acquaintances and other collateral sources when the resulting information is likely to be relevant."[5]

Collateral references can be critical to the evaluator's ability to put the data collected via interview, observation and questionnaire in perspective. This includes collecting the observations and opinions of parties' personal references, extended family and neighbors. Third party professional references (e.g., doctors, therapists) can be at least as valuable (and often more so) but are not directly relevant to this discussion.

For all of their potential value, personal references provided by parties are predictably biased. Although many prove to be genuinely interested in serving the child's needs rather than taking sides in the adult matter, they were undoubtedly selected primarily to bolster the parties' respective positions. Thus, the evaluator is forced to separate the wheat from the chaff: How to distinguish reliable and relevant data from empty and self-serving words.

The challenge inherent in this task has prompted some to recommend that collecting personal references is not worthwhile (e.g., Ackerman, 2006; Bow & Quinnell, 2004). Hynan (2014) takes a more balanced perspective, recommending that references must be "…assertively guided…" so as to minimize delivery of empty even if "glowing" reviews. He recommends careful education of references, structured questions and an emphasis on the report of first-hand reports rather than repetition of third-hand stories.

---

[5] Access the full text at: http://www.apa.org/practice/guidelines/child-custody.aspx.

I find that reaching out to personal references helps to quell parties' anxiety and, done right, can yield valuable data, albeit limited and often time inefficient. In the interest of making the process more time- and therefore cost-efficient, I established the two questionnaires introduced below.

The "**Identifying Resources and References**" questionnaire is delivered to parties prior to the start of evaluation as part of a preliminary paperwork package to be completed prior to initial meetings (i.e., front-loaded). This particular instrument constitutes my first step identifying and organizing all the data to follow, and helps to structure the larger evaluation process. It requests that the respondent provide his or her own contact data in addition to identifying and providing contact data for a number of professional collaterals and as many as three personal references.

A separate page is assigned to each identified reference and is accompanied by a brief informed consent and confidentiality notice. The reader is strongly advised to consult with counsel regarding the legal adequacy of these statements in any given jurisdiction. In some circumstances, a more complete informed consent will be necessary.

The "**Identifying Resources and References**" questionnaire concludes with a sample letter that parties can choose to deliver to the references they identify so as to alert them that the evaluator may soon be in touch.

Upon return receipt of each party's personal reference identifying data, I prepare a "**Voluntary Adult Reference Form**" to deliver to each. I prepare a formal letter for the professional references and assure that I have received and enclosed copies of BOTH parties' consents.

"**Voluntary Adult Reference Form**" clarifies the nature of the matter and the reason for the request. It reminds the recipient he or she has no obligation to respond and will suffer no penalty if he or she chooses not to, and invites completion and return of all or part of the two pages that follow.

The two subsequent pages are identical. The respondent is asked to identify one of the two parties on the first and the other on the second and to answer five questions about each. Additional comments, pages and information are welcomed. Perhaps most critically, the respondent is asked whether follow-up discussion is welcome. Although occasionally a respondent will decline to complete this form at all or expresses a preference to speak by phone, instead, I have never had a respondent refuse to receive a follow-up call. Whether to follow-up with a respondent thereafter depends entirely on the nature of the evaluation and the potential value of his or her contribution.

Standardizing the process using these two instruments helps to make the organizational task more manageable, gratifies parties who are eager for their stories to be heard, and provides the evaluator with the preliminary data that can help to separate the wheat from the chaff.

Identifying Resources and References
© 1990-2013 Benjamin D. Garber Ph.D.

Caregivers: In the course of conducting a family systems evaluation, it is often important to obtain information from concerned others. Please indicate the contact information of all parties identified below.

By providing this information and signing each individual informed consent line, you are legally releasing the evaluator to contact each individual and agency identified here exclusively for the purpose of obtaining information relevant to the present evaluation.

Please complete each page in full and return this original directly to the evaluator. Please contact the individuals and agencies that you identify in these pages to alert them that the evaluator may be in touch soon. Feel free to use the letter on the last page of the document for that purpose, if you wish.

This form is being completed regarding: _____
[child or children's name(s)]

Contacting You

Your Full Name:	
Your home address:	
Your home phone: (___) ___ *Try this number first?*	
Your cell phone: (___) ___ *Try this number first?*	
Name and address of your employer:	
Your work phone: (___) ___ *Try this number first?*	
Your e-mail address:	_____ @ _____ . ___
The best times and days of the week to reach you are:	

This information is typically available prior to the return of this form, but it is often scattered across documents and can be challenging to track down.

It is prudent to alert parties that electronic communications are not secure and to obtain their written acknowledgement of any associated risk (e.g., Sude, 2013; Herlihy, & Corey, 2015).

In particular, beware that if you plan to e-mail both parties simultaneously, you may be trespassing on efforts to protect one's address from the other and associated court orders. In this more and more frequent case, I ask parties to establish a unique e-mail address only for the purpose of the evaluation.

Does HIPAA allow electronic communications?

See www.HHS.gov and

Note A in the following reference section.

FORM 1: Identifying Resources and References
Page 2 of 11

I, (please print your name:) _____ release

_____, to obtain information regarding my child(ren)
(evaluator)

Child's Full Name	Child's Date of Birth
Child's Full Name	Child's Date of Birth
Child's Full Name	Child's Date of Birth

From the following person(s) or agencies:

Child's School

Counselor's Full Name:	
Teacher's Full Name:	
School Name:	
Mailing Address:	
Mailing Address:	
Phone Number:	( )

This release only allows the identified person(s) or agency to provide information to the evaluator for the purpose of informing an on-going court-related matter. This release is inclusive of all information, including drug and alcohol status and HIV/AIDS status, applicable restrictive laws notwithstanding. This release expires upon closure of the present investigation and can be withdrawn at any time by written request to all parties.

_____   _____
Please sign your name   Today's Date

_____
Please indicate your relation to the child(ren)

Resources and References   page 2

Can both parents identify the child's school, teacher(s), principal and counselor?

What does this mean about involvement in the child's life?

Beware that schools may partition a child's record by sections, e.g., grades, behavior, health, special education.

If I receive a record that appears incomplete or otherwise have questions, my first call is to the child's school counselor.

The confidentiality of academic records is bound by FERPA (see NOTE B in references).

FORM 1: Identifying Resources and References
Page 3 of 11

I, (please print your name:) _____ release

_____, to obtain information regarding my child(ren):
(evaluator)

Child's Full Name	Child's Date of Birth
Child's Full Name	Child's Date of Birth
Child's Full Name	Child's Date of Birth

From the following person(s) or agencies:

Child's Pediatrician

Doctor's Full Name:	
Practice Name:	
Mailing Address:	
Mailing Address:	
Phone Number:	( )

This release only allows the identified person(s) or agency to provide information to the evaluator for the purpose of informing an on-going court-related matter. This release is inclusive of all information, including drug and alcohol status and HIV/AIDS status, applicable restrictive laws notwithstanding. This release expires upon closure of the present investigation and can be withdrawn at any time by written request to all parties.

_____   _____
Please sign your name   Today's Date

_____
Please indicate your relation to the child(ren)

Resources and References   page 3

Pediatric and related medical care notes not only document illness, injury and general health status, they often report who accompanies the child to care and describe that adult's demeanor.

I, (please print your name:) _____ release

_____, to obtain information regarding my child(ren):
(evaluator)

Child's Full Name	Child's Date of Birth
Child's Full Name	Child's Date of Birth
Child's Full Name	Child's Date of Birth

From the following person(s) or agencies:

Child's Psychotherapist	Psychotherapist's Full Name:	
	Group or Agency Name:	
	Mailing Address:	
	Mailing Address:	
	Phone Number:	( )

This release only allows the identified person(s) or agency to provide information to the evaluator for the purpose of informing an on-going court-related matter. This release is inclusive of all information, including drug and alcohol status and HIV/AIDS status, applicable restrictive laws notwithstanding. This release expires upon closure of the present investigation and can be withdrawn at any time by written request to all parties.

_____   _____
Please sign your name   Today's Date

_____
Please indicate your relation to the child(ren)

Resources and References   page 4

Accessing a child's psychotherapy notes and/or talking to the child's psychotherapist in some instances may compromise the child's felt-safety in that therapy or parties' subsequent endorsement of that therapist as child-centered.

Some jurisdictions have codified protections intended to serve the child's right to psychotherapy.
See e.g., Berg v. Berg (NH Supreme Court http://www.courts.state.nh.us/supreme/opinions/2005/berg112.htm):

"We conclude that parents do not have the exclusive right to assert or waive the privilege on their child's behalf."

I, (please print your name:) _____ release

_____, to obtain information regarding my child(ren):
(evaluator)

Child's Full Name	Child's Date of Birth
Child's Full Name	Child's Date of Birth
Child's Full Name	Child's Date of Birth

From the following person(s) or agencies:

Child's	Full Name:	
	Full Name:	
	Agency Name:	
	Mailing Address:	
	Mailing Address:	
	Phone Number:	( )

This release only allows the identified person(s) or agency to provide information to the evaluator for the purpose of informing an on-going court-related matter. This release is inclusive of all information, including drug and alcohol status and HIV/AIDS status, applicable restrictive laws notwithstanding. This release expires upon closure of the present investigation and can be withdrawn at any time by written request to all parties.

_____   _____
Please sign your name   Today's Date

_____
Please indicate your relation to the child(ren)

Resources and References   page 5

This blank child-related page often elicits identification of relevant informants that may not otherwise have been identified early on in the process.

FORM 1: Identifying Resources and References
Page 6-7 of 11

I, (please print your name:) _____ release

_____, to obtain infor
(evaluator)

Your Psychotherapist	Psychotherapist's Full Name:	
	Group or Agency Name:	
	Mailing Address:	
	Mailing Address:	
	Phone Number:	( )

This release only allows the identified person(s) or agency to provide inf
purpose of informing an on-going court-related matter. This release
including drug and alcohol status and HIV/AIDS status, applicable restr
release expires upon closure of the present investigation and can be w
request to all parties.

_____   _____
Please sign your name

Resources and References

I, (please print your name:) _____ release

_____, to obtain information regarding my child(ren):
(evaluator)

Your Present Employer	Employer's Full Name:	
	Alternate Contact Person:	
	Company Name:	
	Mailing Address:	
	Mailing Address:	
	Phone Number:	( )
	Employed here beginning (month/year):	

This release only allows the identified person(s) or agency to provide information to the evaluator for the purpose of informing an on-going court-related matter. This release is inclusive of all information, including drug and alcohol status and HIV/AIDS status, applicable restrictive laws notwithstanding. This release expires upon closure of the present investigation and can be withdrawn at any time by written request to all parties.

_____   _____
Please sign your name   Today's Date

Resources and References   page 7

Some parties may resist involving employers for fear of compromising the workplace. Determine first whether any relevant data is likely to be gleaned by this request.

Beware that parties' psychotherapists can become triangulated into the family conflict easily, particularly when their only source of information is their individual client.

FORM 1: Identifying Resources and References
Pages 8-10 of 11

I, (please print your name:) _____ release

_____, to obtain information regarding my child(ren):
(evaluator)

Your Personal Reference

Individual's Full Name:	
Mailing Address:	
Mailing Address:	
Phone Number:	( )
Phone Number:	( )
Phone Number:	( )

This release only allows the identified person(s) or agency to provide information to the evaluator for the purpose of informing an on-going court-related matter. This release is inclusive of all information, including drug and alcohol status and HIV/AIDS status, applicable restrictive laws notwithstanding. This release expires upon closure of the present investigation and can be withdrawn at any time by written request to all parties.

_____   _____
Please sign your name   Today's Date

R1

I, (please print your name:) _____ release

_____, to obtain information regarding my child(ren):
(evaluator)

Your Personal Reference

Individual's Full Name:	
Mailing Address:	
Mailing Address:	
Phone Number:	( )
Phone Number:	

Resources and References

to provide information to the evaluator for the This release is inclusive of all information, plicable restrictive laws notwithstanding. This nd can be withdrawn at any time by written

_____
Today's Date

R2

page 9

I, (please print your name:) _____ release

_____, to obtain information regarding my child(ren):
(evaluator)

Your Personal Reference

Individual's Full Name:	
Mailing Address:	
Mailing Address:	
Phone Number:	( )
Phone Number:	( )
Phone Number:	( )

This release only allows the identified person(s) or agency to provide information to the evaluator for the purpose of informing an on-going court-related matter. This release is inclusive of all information, including drug and alcohol status and HIV/AIDS status, applicable restrictive laws notwithstanding. This release expires upon closure of the present investigation and can be withdrawn at any time by written request to all parties.

_____   _____
Please sign your name   Today's Date

R3

Resources and References   page 10

Dear _____,

I am writing to alert you that _____ (evaluator's name) may soon contact you about my family. The evaluator is conducting a family systems evaluation with my consent. His/her job is to learn as much about our family as possible in order to help make decisions in the kids' best interests.

I will very much appreciate your time and effort speaking to the evaluator. Please feel free to share anything that you choose, as openly and honestly as possible. Feel free to contact him or her at the number below with any questions or concerns.

With gratitude for your assistance in helping the kids, I am,

Sincerely,

_____

_____
(evaluator's full name and credentials)

_____
(evaluator's contact information)

Resources and References   page 11

I am seldom aware whether parties use this format to alert their references to the process. As often as not, super-compliant parents sign this page and return it as if it were another questionnaire.

I introduced the page initially in response to an anxious parent's questions about how to tell her friends that she was asking for their support.

FORM 2: Voluntary Adult Reference Form
Page 1 of 3

**Voluntary
Adult Reference Form**

In the matter of:

In the best interests of:

You have been identified as a valuable source of information relevant to this family's current litigation. Your time and effort replying to each of the following questions may be very helpful in the process of determining how best to serve these children's needs.

Your response to this inquiry is entirely voluntary. You may refuse to respond to any or all of this inquiry at your discretion and entirely without consequence. If you decide to respond, please understand that the information that you share will not be kept confidential. It may be incorporated into a report regarding the children's needs which will come before the court.

Please feel free to elaborate on any question raised in this document and to add any additional thoughts, observations, concerns or recommendations on the reverse or on a separate page, as you see fit.

Please reach me at any time if you have questions or concerns.

With gratitude for any contribution that you choose to make, I am,

_____
(evaluator)

Please sign here acknowledging that you understand that the information that you provide will be treated with discretion but is neither confidential nor privileged. It may be shared as part of the pending litigation.

_____
Your signature   Today's Date

The evaluator is obliged to assure that any potential reference is fully informed about the conditions under which the inquiry is being made including the fact that compliance is voluntary and that anything he or she chooses to offer is not protected.

FORM 2: Voluntary Adult Reference Form
Page 2-3 of 3

Print your name: _____ page 2

Please answer the following five questions about one parent. This person is: _____
Please print his or her name

1. How do you know this individual? How and when did you meet? In what role or circumstances do you see one another?

Print your name: _____ page 3

Please answer the next five questions about the *other* parent. This person is: _____
Please print his or her name

6. How do you know this individual? How and when did you meet? In what role or circumstances do you see one another?

2. How v
exam]

3. How v
exam]

7. How would you describe this person's strengths? Please offer examples:

8. How would you describe this person's weaknesses? Please offer examples:

4. How v
his/he

5. Is this

9. Please describe the other parent's parenting strengths and weaknesses:

10. Is this person....?
_____ True?   a. Ever violent, intentionally destructive or threatening?
_____ True?   b. Ever impaired by substances (Alcohol? Drugs?)
_____ True?   c. Ever inappropriate around children?
_____ True?   d. Ever intellectually or emotionally limited or impaired?

Please feel free to offer any additional thoughts or comments on the reverse.

| May I reach you if I have additional questions? _____ YES _____ NO |
| If YES, at what number: _____ When? _____ |

I find that the least useful personal references only know one parent.

Any TRUE responses require careful follow-up.

Can the respondent provide specific, first-hand examples?

Why don't these pages ask the respondent to comment on the child?

If a respondent has first-hand experience with the child, the relevant data can be voluminous and quite sensitive. I believe that such data is more appropriately and thoroughly obtained in interview.

References

Ackerman, Mark J. (2006). *Clinician's guide to child custody evaluations* (3rd ed.). Hoboken, NJ, US: John Wiley & Sons Inc.

American Psychological Association. (APA; 2010). Guidelines for child custody evaluations in family law proceedings. *American Psychologist*, 65, 863-867.

Bow, J. N. Quinnell, F. A. (2004). Critique of child custody evaluations by the legal profession. *Family Court Review*, 42, 115-127.

Herlihy, Barbara; Corey, G. (2015). *Boundary issues in counseling: Multiple roles and responsibilities* (3rd ed.). Alexandria, VA, US: American Counseling Association.

Hynan, D. (2014). *Child Custody Evaluations*. Charles C. Thomas: Springfield, Illinois.

Sude, M. E. (2013). Text messaging and private practice: Ethical challenges and guidelines for developing personal best practices. *Journal of Mental Health Counseling*, 35, 211-227.

NOTE A: HIPAA and electronic communications:

The Privacy Rule allows covered health care providers to communicate electronically, such as through e-mail, with their patients, provided they apply reasonable safeguards when doing so. See 45 C.F.R. § 164.530(c).

For example, certain precautions may need to be taken when using e-mail to avoid unintentional disclosures, such as checking the e-mail address for accuracy before sending, or sending an e-mail alert to the patient for address confirmation prior to sending the message.

Further, while the Privacy Rule does not prohibit the use of unencrypted e-mail for treatment-related communications between health care providers and patients, other safeguards should be applied to reasonably protect privacy, such as limiting the amount or type of information disclosed through the unencrypted e-mail.

In addition, covered entities will want to ensure that any transmission of electronic protected health information is in compliance with the HIPAA Security Rule requirements at 45 C.F.R. Part 164, Subpart C. Note that an individual has the right under the Privacy Rule to request and have a covered health care provider communicate with him or her by alternative means or at alternative locations, if reasonable. See 45 C.F.R. § 164.522(b).

Accessed 01.17.2015 from:

http://www.hhs.gov/ocr/privacy/hipaa/faq/health_information_technology/570.html

NOTE B: The Family Education Rights and Privacy Act (FERPA) can be found at: http://www2.ed.gov/policy/gen/reg/ferpa/index.html

§99.30   Under what conditions is prior consent required to disclose information?

(a) The parent or eligible student shall provide a signed and dated written consent before an educational agency or institution discloses personally identifiable information from the student's education records, except as provided in §99.31.

(b) The written consent must:

    (1) Specify the records that may be disclosed;

    (2) State the purpose of the disclosure; and

    (3) Identify the party or class of parties to whom the disclosure may be made.

(c) When a disclosure is made under paragraph (a) of this section:

    (1) If a parent or eligible student so requests, the educational agency or institution shall provide him or her with a copy of the records disclosed; and

    (2) If the parent of a student who is not an eligible student so requests, the agency or institution shall provide the student with a copy of the records disclosed.

(d) "Signed and dated written consent" under this part may include a record and signature in electronic form that—

    (1) Identifies and authenticates a particular person as the source of the electronic consent; and

    (2) Indicates such person's approval of the information contained in the electronic consent.

B. Caregiver History and Perspectives

Rationale and uses

The family law professional charged with advising the court in matters concerned with a child's well-being is ethically obligated to consider the historical context of the matter at hand (AFCC, 2007; APA, 2010; King, 2013). This includes collecting and/or creating a chronology of events relevant to the present evaluation and a history from each caregiver (e.g., Gould & Martindale, 2007; Hynan, 2014).

Collecting a chronology in advance of interview serves at least two purposes. The process of preparing a chronology helps the participant-caregiver put events in sequence so as to discuss cause-effect questions more succinctly and clearly. Review of participants' chronologies helps the evaluator to target critical incidents, discrepancies and distortions as compared to third party records such as court orders, police and child protective reports and school or therapy notes. The "**Chronology of Critical Events Worksheet**" is provided on page 25 for distribution to caregivers so as to facilitate their report of immediate history.

But the relevant history goes far beyond immediate events. Custody litigants, for example, are inclined to begin their chronologies with the first adult separation or at the time of divorce. The history setting the stage for the instant evaluation goes back at least as far as each caregiver's own childhood. For this purpose, the "**Individual Caregiver Personal and Parenting History**" questionnaire is provided on page 27.

The "**Individual Caregiver Personal and Parenting History**" questionnaire asks caregivers to succinctly summarize their experience of their own parents and their own parents' relationship with one another. For better or worse, we know that these early experiences can predispose our adult choices.

We know, for example, that an individual's experience of parenting and family relationships can shape their own parenting practices and relationships as an adult. Perhaps the most startling illustration of this observation is evident in Mary Main's often replicated observation that pregnant mothers' descriptions of their own childhoods strongly predict the quality of their relationships with their yet-to-be born children well beyond the child's first year (e.g., Behrens, Hesse & Main, 2007).

We also know that early experiences of abuse, neglect and trauma can resonate negatively in adulthood (e.g., Conger et al., 2013; Merrick, Leeb & Lee, 2013; Schofield, Lee & Merrick, 2013).

The literature demonstrating the link between one's childhood experience of parenting and the quality of subsequent relationships is diverse and compelling. Parade, Supple and Helms (2012) summarize: "Children reared in environments characterized by more warmth and less harsh parenting develop a more positive lens through which they view the world around them and come to expect that their interactions with others will be pleasant and enjoyable"(p. 151).

The "**Individual Caregiver Personal and Parenting History**" questionnaire goes further to survey the caregiver's history and present functioning in several specific areas. These include: overviews of the individual's medical, academic, addictions, mental health, relationship and legal histories. Each such area invites the participant to flag areas that may be of concern to the evaluator for subsequent exploration.

The "**Individual Caregiver Personal and Parenting History**" questionnaire closes with a number of critical questions about the respondent's priorities and parenting practices. I have often found the final page of this resource especially valuable, "**My Priorities**."

"**My Priorities**" asks caregivers to rank order the importance of fifteen value statements. The task requires careful consideration of one's professed investment in self versus child versus material comforts. This tool, like all the others provided in this volume, has no right or wrong answers. Instead, caregiver responses can be compared to those of co-parents, to history and to direct observations so as to better understand how each adult has in the past and may in the future invest their finite time, effort and money. Because the task forces choices among competing interests (just like life), responses can be very revealing.

FORM 3: Chronology of Critical Events Worksheet
Page 1 of 2

Chronology of Critical Events Worksheet

Please use this form to create a concise history of events leading up to the present investigation. Begin at or before the start of the adult relationship and highlight relevant events (e.g., relocation, birth of a child, separations, therapies) through the present. Copy the next page to add additional pages.

Completed by: _____ Today's Date: _____ page # _____

Approximate time/date/span	Location	Describe Event (Bulleted item)	Your comments
Example: June, 1999	Oshkosh, WI	House fire – lost everything	Caused much anxiety, many arguments; Dad blamed me; beloved pet iguana "Fido" died in fire; relocated to my parents house x6 months while we rebuilt.
distant			
present			

Next page

Respondent is asked first to identify a "critical event" objectively by date and place

Respondent is invited to offer a subjective impression of the meaning of event, e.g., how is this relevant to evaluation?

Respondent is directed to record events from most distant to most current in sequence.

FORM 3: Chronology of Critical Events Worksheet
Page 2 of 2

The respondent is invited to copy page two as many times as necessary to include all relevant events.

Chronology of Critical Events Worksheet Administration and interpretation:

1. Respondents sometimes find the request to organize and sequence a long and painful history quite overwhelming. It is not unusual for parties to report that completing the chronology and associated paperwork recreated the distress like a post-traumatic stress. Alert to this, the evaluator reasonably allows participants to take their time, completing one bit at a time as time and stress allow.[6]

2. Respondents who need further assistance can be directed to record events on individual notecards, shuffled into reverse order (most distant to most current) and then transcribed onto the form.

3. Which events respondents identify as relevant and include in the chronology can be revealing. An event included by one parent but not the other may be reason to inquire further of both. Among the relevant hypotheses are questions as to whether the parent who omitted the event is prone to denial and avoidance more generally and/or whether the parent who included the event is trying to emphasize matters so as to demean the other parent or win the evaluator's sympathies.

---

[6] Participating in a court-ordered evaluation can recreate traumatic stress for some individuals. Common as this observation is, there is no professional literature on the subject.

Individual Caregiver
Personal and Parenting History
© Benjamin D. Garber, Ph.D.

This questionnaire has been prepared to facilitate review of your personal history as part of the present assessment. Your full and complete responses will help to make this process more time and cost efficient. Please feel free to elaborate on any response on the reverse of any page or on separate pages appended to this questionnaire.

Please return this original questionnaire upon completion directly to Dr. Garber.

Thank you, in advance, for your time and effort.

Who is completing this form: _____
(your name)

_____   _____
(your relationship to the child[ren])   (your date of birth)

Family of Origin

1. I am adopted or for other reasons   YES ☐   NO ☐
know little or nothing about my BIOLOGICAL relatives

2. I grew up with:

Full Name	Present age	Biological/legal relationship to you	Living where or died when?	Is this person a support to you in the present?

(Parents or caregivers / Brothers/sisters/other relatives)

> Pages 1 - 4 concern the respondent's family of origin

> Parents who were adopted and have little or no knowledge of their biological origins and/or have a history of multiple placements can pose special challenges both to the evaluator who values that background and to the adult as a parent (e.g., Klahr & Burt, 2014).

FORM 4: Individual Caregiver Personal and Parenting History
Pages 2 and 3 of 14

Caregiver Personal History   page 3

Your Name: _____   Today's Date: _____

My "MOTHER" refers to the primary female caregiver I grew up with,
no matter her legal or biological relationship to me or to my father:

5. Growing up, my mother was...

a. I had no primary female caregiver or "Mother" growing up ☐ YES ☐ NO

(If YES, please skip to #7)

b. ...a kind and supportive parent ☐ YES ☐ NO

c. ...a firm and consistent parent ☐ YES ☐ NO

d. ...a good role model ☐ YES ☐ NO

e. ...a hard worker and a good provider ☐ YES ☐ NO

f. ...a good partner to my father ☐ YES ☐ NO

g. ...my best friend ☐ YES ☐ NO

h. ...my only friend ☐ YES ☐ NO

i. ... violent or abusive (physically, verbally or sexually) to me ☐ YES ☐ NO

Do parents of the child's gender have a bigger impact on that child's parenting behaviors as an adult? (e.g., Parke 2013)

Caregiver Personal History   page 3

Your Name: _____   Today's Date: _____

My "MOTHER" refers to the primary female caregiver I grew up with,
no matter her legal or biological relationship to me or to my father:

5. Growing up, my mother was...

a. I had no primary female caregiver or "Mother" growing up ☐ YES ☐ NO

(If YES, please skip to #7)

b. ...a kind and supportive parent ☐ YES ☐ NO

c. ...a firm and consistent parent ☐ YES ☐ NO

d. ...a good role model ☐ YES ☐ NO

e. ...a hard worker and a good provider ☐ YES ☐ NO

f. ...a good partner to my father ☐ YES ☐ NO

g. ...my best friend ☐ YES ☐ NO

h. ...my only friend ☐ YES ☐ NO

i. ... violent or abusive (physically, verbally or sexually) to me ☐ YES ☐ NO

j. ... violent or abusive (physically, verbally or sexually) to my brothers and/or sisters ☐ YES ☐ NO

k. ... violent or abusive (physically, verbally or sexually) to my father or other adults ☐ YES ☐ NO

l. ... alcoholic, drug-dependent or otherwise a substance abuser or addict ☐ YES ☐ NO

m. ... passive and uninvolved ☐ YES ☐ NO

n. ... inconsistent and unpredictable one day to the next ☐ YES ☐ NO

o. ... NOT supportive of my father, often undermined him ☐ YES ☐ NO

p. My mother remains an active participant in my child(ren)'s lives ☐ YES ☐ NO

6. Is your experience of your mother when you were a child relevant to your own parenting and/or the state of your marriage? If so, how:

© Benjamin D. Garber, Ph.D.   www.healthyparent.com

Do parents who grew up with violence find themselves in violent adult relationships? (e.g., Finzi-Dottan &Harel, 2014; Jennings et al., 2014)

Grandparents who are active in their grandchildren's lives are often valuable contributors (and are sometimes active co-parents) relevant to evaluation.

Caregiver Personal History   page 4

Your Name: _____   Today's Date: _____

"MY PARENT'S RELATIONSHIP" describes how
the adults who raised me got along with each other when I was a child
no matter the legal status of their relationship and regardless of whether they lived together.

7.   My parents' relationship ...

a. ...was good: they consistently cooperated and communicated
   and supported one another even though the hard times   ☐ YES   ☐ NO

b. ...always put my needs first   ☐ YES   ☐ NO

c. ...was unpredictable; it was on and off over time ... I often feared
   that they would split up   ☐ YES   ☐ NO

d. ...was troubled; I had to do things to try to keep them together   ☐ YES   ☐ NO

e. ...was troubled; they communicated through me   ☐ YES   ☐ NO

f. ...was troubled; they treated me like a peer or an adult even
   while I was a child   ☐ YES   ☐ NO

g. ...was troubled; it was like living in a war zone   ☐ YES   ☐ NO

h. ...was troubled; I never knew who could be there or how they
   would get along one day to the next   ☐ YES   ☐ NO

i. ...ended in separation or divorce   ☐ YES   ☐ NO
                                                              If NO then skip to #8

j. ...ended peacefully and civilly; they cooperated and made sure
   my needs were met   ☐ YES   ☐ NO

k. ...ended in conflict   ☐ YES   ☐ NO

l. ...ended in a battle over custody of me and/or my brothers and/or
   sisters   ☐ YES   ☐ NO

m. ...ended because of my father   ☐ YES   ☐ NO

n. ...ended because of my mother   ☐ YES   ☐ NO

o. ...ended because of me or something I did   ☐ YES   ☐ NO

8.   Is your experience of your parents' relationship when you were a child
relevant to your own parenting and/or the state of your marriage? If so, how:

© Benjamin D. Garber, Ph.D.   www.healthyparent.com

> Adultified and parentified children are at high risk for later dysfunction, including enlisting their children as their allies and caregivers (e.g., Garber, 2011).

FORM 4: Individual Caregiver Personal and Parenting History
Page 5 of 14

Your Name: _____   Today's Date: _____

My Medical History

9. Please use this table to identify any illness, injury, surgery or other medical procedure you've experienced or are anticipating in the future.

Identify the illness, injury, surgery or procedure by name	Date completed or anticipated	Name of physician or other responsible provider	How does this affect you in the present?
(a)			
(b)			
(c)			
(d)			

Please use the reverse side to continue. Please attach copies of any documents (medical notes, prescription copies) that might help to explain.

10. Medications I am presently taking:

Name of medication	Dosage	Name of prescribing physician	I take this medication because...
(a)			
(b)			
(c)			
(d)			

There is no a priori reason to assume that any specific medical problem or medication limits an individual's parenting capacity. Any acknowledged condition or medication must be explored, however, as to its impact on strength, stamina, alertness and thinking, mood, energy level and fatigue and similar variables:

"How does this impact you day to day?"

"Did you take it today?"

Chronic and degenerative conditions may require particular focus (e.g.,O'Donnell et al., 2013).

FORM 4: Individual Caregiver Personal and Parenting History
Page 6 of 14

Caregiver Personal History   page 6

Your Name: _____ Today's Date: _____

Academic History

11. I am currently a student   YES ☐   NO ☐
                                      If YES please describe on reverse

12. The highest grade or level I have successfully completed to date is:

☐ Less than 12th ☐ High School/GED ☐ College ☐ Advanced Degree: _____

13. In school, my grades were generally:

Elementary School	A B C D F		High School	A B C D F
Junior High/ Middle School	A B C D F		College +	A B C D F

14. Looking back, I now believe that ...

a. ...I had/have a learning disability that interfered with grades   ☐ YES   ☐ NO

b. ...I had/have an attention problem (e.g., ADD or ADHD) that interfered with grades   ☐ YES   ☐ NO

c. ...I should have tried harder   ☐ YES   ☐ NO

d. ...I have/had speech/language, OT, PT, vision or hearing problem that interfered with grades   ☐ YES   ☐ NO

e. ...I was/am depressed and this interfered with grades   ☐ YES   ☐ NO

f. ...I had/have emotional problems get in the way of my learning   ☐ YES   ☐ NO

g. ...I was/am anxious and this interfered with grades   ☐ YES   ☐ NO

h. ...I had/have a substance abuse problem (e.g., drugs or alcohol) that got in the way of grades   ☐ YES   ☐ NO

15. As an adult,

a. ...I care about education deeply   ☐ YES   ☐ NO

b. ...I like to read   ☐ YES   ☐ NO

c. ...I am involved with my children's school   ☐ YES   ☐ NO

d. ...I attend activities at my children's school   ☐ YES   ☐ NO

© Benjamin D. Garber, Ph.D.   www.healthyparent.com

A parent's academic achievement has some predictive value on the child's academic achievement (e.g., Chi, 2013; Pears et al., 2013).

If ADD or ADHD is identified here, was it also identified on page 5 ("Medical")?

Why not?

I have never yet seen a parent deny being deeply invested in his or her child's education.

The question remains because it opens discussion of the discrepancy when there is little objective evidence that the parent helps with homework, attends conferences and such.

Parents' actual reading practices predict children's reading and academics

(see e.g., Yeo, Ong & Ng, 2014).

FORM 4: Individual Caregiver Personal and Parenting History
Page 7 of 14

Your Name: _____ Today's Date: _____

Addictive Behaviors

16. Please indicate which of the following are TRUE to the best of your knowledge:

Please detail all YES responses on the reverse

	EVER TRUE about me?	EVER TRUE someone related to you?

ALCOHOL USE (including beer, mixed drinks and others)
a. Consume ANY alcoholic beverages at all
b. Consider alcohol consumption to EVER impair work, relationships, parenting
c. EVER been charged, arrested, indicted for a crime under the influence (includes DWI, DUI) of alcohol

PRESCRIPTION MEDICATIONS:
d. Consume ANY prescription medications in the past ONE YEAR
e. Consider prescription medications to EVER impair work, relationships, parenting
f. EVER been charged, arrested, indicted for a crime under the influence (includes DWI, DUI) of prescription medications

OVER THE COUNTER (OTC) MEDICATIONS (e.g. Aspirin, Tylenol, diet pills)
g. Consume ANY OTC medications in the past ONE YEAR
h. Consider OTC medications to EVER impair work, relationships, parenting
i. EVER been charged, arrested, indicted for a crime under the influence (includes DWI, DUI) of OTC medications

GAMBLING, GAMING, SPENDING/SHOPPING, INTERNET and/or VIDEO
j. EVER engage in these activities?
k. Consider these activities to EVER impair work, relationships, parenting
l. EVER been charged, arrested, indicted for a crime related to these activities

PORNOGRAPHY, SEXUAL ADDICTIONS/COMPULSIONS
m. EVER engage in these activities?
n. Consider these activities to EVER impair work, relationships, parenting
o. EVER been charged, arrested, indicted for a crime related to these activities

Please explain all YES responses on the reverse

© Benjamin D. Garber, Ph.D.   www.healthyparent.com

Parental attitudes and practices regarding drugs and alcohol influence children's behavior through high school (e.g., Stafström, 2014).

Villalta et al (2014) discuss the association between "affectionless control" among addicted parents including gamblers.

Read more about the children of substance abusing parents (e.g., Itäpuisto, 2014) and the mediating role of co-parenting (e.g., Kachadourian et al., 2009).

FORM 4: Individual Caregiver Personal and Parenting History

Caregiver Personal History   page 8

Your Name: _____   Today's Date: _____

Mental Health History

17. Please indicate which of the following are TRUE to the best of your knowledge:

Please detail all YES responses on the reverse

	EVER TRUE about myself?	EVER TRUE about someone related to the you?
a. Anxious, nervous, worried, fearful		
b. Perfectionistic, self-critical or critical of others		
c. Depressed; feels hopeless, helpless or worthless		
d. Self-destructive, suicidal		
e. Violent, abusive and/or destructive of property		
f. Psychotic, schizophrenic, delusional or paranoid		
g. Trauma survivor, PTSD		
h. Multiple personality or dissociative identity		
i. Eating disorder: Binging, purging, hoarding food		
j. Alcohol, drug or other substance use, abuse, dependence		
k. Referred to but refused counseling, psychotherapy or psychological treatment of any kind		
l. Been in counseling, psychotherapy or psychological treatment of any kind		
m. Completed psychological, neuropsychological or psychiatric testing or assessment of any kind		
n. Prescribed psycho-active or psychotropic medication for any period (examples: Ritalin, Xanax, Prozac, Zoloft)		
o. Hospitalized due to psychological, psychiatric or substance abuse concerns		
p. Parenting impaired by psychological, psychiatric or substance abuse concern		
q. Co-parenting impaired by psychological, psychiatric or substance abuse concern		
r. Fulfilling responsibilities as a husband, wife or partner in an intimate relationship impaired by psychological, psychiatric or substance abuse concern		
s. Employment or public responsibilities impaired by psychological, psychiatric or substance abuse concern		

Please explain all YES responses on the reverse

© Benjamin D. Garber, Ph.D.   www.healthyparent.com

Here again, within the limits of safety, mental illness has no necessary bearing on parenting or child outcomes.

What matters are symptoms, not labels.

(see also Ackerson, 2003)

Trauma? Was the child exposed? Does the parent's PTSD impact parenting? Among vets, for example: "symptoms of PTSD and depression may be related to increased symptomatology in children and problems with parenting ..."

(Creech et al., 2014)

Beware that administering psychological tests as part of a child-centered forensic family evaluation risks doing more harm than good
(e.g., AFCC, 2007; Garber, 2009; King, 2013).

FORM 4: Individual Caregiver Personal and Parenting History
Page 9 of 14

Your Name: _____   Today's Date: _____

History of Crime and Conviction

18. Please indicate which of the following are TRUE to the best of your knowledge:

Please detail all YES responses on the reverse

		EVER TRUE about myself?	EVER TRUE about someone related to you?
a.	Convicted of a misdemeanor?		
b.	Convicted of a felony?		
c.	Convicted of a violent crime of any kind?		
d.	Found guilty of Driving While Intoxicated (DWI or DWD)		
e.	Found guilty of child abuse or neglect?		
f.	Ever served time in jail or prison?		
g.	Ever been on probation?		
h.	Ever had driver's license revoked?		
i.	Ever been involved in any legal action EXCLUDING the present divorce/custody action		
j.	Ever been subject to a restraining order?		
k.	Ever filed bankruptcy?		
l.	Ever been identified as a sexual offender?		
m.	Ever sued or been sued by anyone?		

Please explain the YES responses on the reverse

© Benjamin D. Garber, Ph.D.   www.healthyparent.com

Is the respondent's self-report consistent with a search of criminal records?

A history of violent crimes and crimes against children will be of grave concern.

When questions of terminating a parent's rights arise, see e.g., Friedman & Evans, 2006.

Regarding incarcerated parents see e.g., Roxburgh & Fitch, 2014.

These hypotheticals are relevant primarily to divorce and divorce-related (e.g., parenting rights and responsibilities, access, contact refusal, relocation) matters. They may not make sense in the context of other litigation (e.g., foster, adoption).

Caregiver Personal History   page 10

Your Name: _____   Today's Date: _____

The Child[ren]'s Point of View

Helping children cope with family stress and transition can be very difficult. There often are no right or wrong answers. Please take time to imagine how you might respond to each of the following situations. Feel free to continue your responses on the reverse.

19. How do you reply if your son or daughter says to you, **"My other parent says that you're mean!"**

20. How do you reply if your son/daughter says to you, **"I want to live with my other parent."**

21. How do you reply if your son or daughter says to you, **"I love you and I hate my other parent."**

22. How do you reply if your son or daughter says to you, **"I'm not going back to stay/visit with my other parent ever!"**

23. How do you reply if your son or daughter says to you, **"My other parent told me to keep something a secret and I can't tell you."**

24. How do you reply if your son or daughter says to you, **"Do you love my other parent?"**

25. How do you reply if your son or daughter says to you, **"If I weren't here you two would still be together!"**

© Benjamin D. Garber, Ph.D.   www.healthyparent.com

These hypotheticals elicit idealized responses and therefore tap parenting strengths and information, but not necessarily real life practices.

At issue are dynamics such as adultification (how much information does the parent share?) and alienation (how does the parent insulate the child from his or her real feelings about the other parent?).

Implicit here is the respondent's empathy versus self-centeredness, and impulse control.

FORM 4: Individual Caregiver Personal and Parenting History
Pages 11 and 12 of 14

Caregiver Personal History   page 11

Your Name: _____   Today's Date: _____

Prior Relationship History

26. Growing up, my best friend was: _____ (name)

27. I began dating at what age: ☐ years old

28. I became sexually active (that is, first had intercourse) at what age: ☐ years old

29. I first lived away from my parent(s) at what age: ☐ years old

30. I first moved away from home at what age: ☐ years old

31. I first lived with (cohabitated with) a sexual partner at what age: ☐ years old

32. I have had many relationships ☑ YES   ☐ NO

33. In general, when my relationships end, I end them ☐ YES   ☐ NO

34. In general, when my relationships end, my partner ends them ☐ YES   ☐ NO

Caregiver Personal History   page 12

Your Name: _____   Today's Date: _____   next page

Present Relationship History

39. My relationship with my estranged partner was EXCLUSIVELY for the purpose of having or raising a child; we never had any other adult-adult relationship. ☐ YES   ☐ NO

40. We began dating: _____ (month/year)

41. We became sexually active (that is, first had intercourse) _____ (month/year)

42. We first lived together: _____ (month/year)

43. We got married: _____ (month/year)

44. I once found this relationship fulfilling ☐ YES   ☐ NO

45. I had imagined this relationship would last forever ☐ YES   ☐ NO

46. We first separated due to conflict: _____ (month/year)

47. This was the ONE AND ONLY separation leading up to the present ☐ YES   ☐ NO
If NO please detail separations/reunions by date on reverse

48. I initiated this separation ☐ YES   ☐ NO

49. I agreed to this separation but it was NOT my wish ☐ YES   ☐ NO

50. I do not want this separation, it is entirely my co-parent's doing ☐ YES   ☐ NO

51. I want to get back together with my child(ren)'s other parent ☐ YES   ☑ NO

52. Legal separation, divorce or custody papers were first filed: _____ (month/year)

53. I have tried to cooperate with my co-parent in ending this relationship ☑ YES   ☐ NO

54. I will fight my co-parent every step of the way for what I feel I deserve ☐ YES   ☐ NO

55. I will fight my co-parent every step of the way for what I feel the child(ren) need ☐ YES   ☐ NO

56. I believe that we should stay together for the sake of the child(ren) no matter what ☐ YES   ☐ NO

© Benjamin D. Garber, Ph.D.   www.healthyparent.com

Have the respondent's adult relationships been stable over time?

How have they ended?

Is there a pattern that might bear on understanding the present adult relationship?

Has the child been introduced to the parent's partners?

Has this created serial unexplained losses when the adults broke up?

What is the child's experience of serial separations? Does the child expect another reunion ahead?

Priorities again:

This can have religious/cultural family-of-origin meaning.

Explore further.

Caregiver Personal History   page 13

Your Name: _____   Today's Date: _____

57. Please identify your own greatest strengths and weaknesses as a parent:

My parenting **strengths**	My parenting **weaknesses**
a.	a.
b.	b.
c.	c.
d.	d.
e.	e.

The children's other parent's parenting **strengths**	The children's other parent's parenting **weaknesses**
a.	a.
b.	b.
c.	c.
d.	d.
e.	e.

© Benjamin D. Garber, Ph.D.   www.healthyparent.com

I find the respondent's willingness and ability to articulate his or her own weaknesses and the other parent's parenting strengths powerful and revealing.

I'm looking for maturity, perspective taking and the ability to put aside emotion in order to recognize the child's needs.

The respondent who can only offer his or her own strengths and only the co-parent's weaknesses may be prone to black and white thinking more generally and unable to support the child's relationship with the other adult.

And then we must ask:

But what if the other adult is objectively dangerous...?

Learn about the real and important distinction between alienation and estrangement

(e.g., Garber, 2004).

FORM 4: Individual Caregiver Personal and Parenting History

Page 14 of 14

Your Name: _____   Today's Date: _____

My Priorities

59. Please rank the following items in order of importance. There are no right or wrong answers.
Please do NOT use partial numbers, fractions or decimals. Rank the items so that ...

1 = Your HIGHEST priority; the one item on the list that is MOST important to you

and

15 = Your LOWEST priority; the one item that is LEAST important to you

- a. My own happiness
- b. My own physical and mental health
- c. A successful co-parenting relationship with my child(ren)'s other parent
- d. My child(ren)'s other parent's happiness
- e. My child(ren)'s other parent's physical and mental health
- f. Finding a new partner or spouse for myself
- g. My child(ren)'s physical and mental health
- h. My child(ren)'s happiness
- i. The quality of my child(ren)'s relationship with me
- j. The quality of my child(ren)'s relationship with their other parent
- k. The quality of my child(ren)'s relationship with my new/future partner or spouse
- l. The quality of my child(ren)'s relationship with their other parent's new/future partner or spouse
- m. My ability to provide for my child(ren) financially
- n. The comfort of the home that I provide for my child(ren)
- o. The amount of time that I'm with my children each week/month

© Benjamin D. Garber, Ph.D.   www.healthyparent.com

This task can stand alone and is sometimes administered as a single page in the context of narrowly defined evaluations or as a tool when working with co-parents. See page 29.

Beware that occasionally a respondent will assign either the number 1 or the number 15 to all items.

Every effort to reword this to date has failed to escape this misunderstanding.

At issue is how the respondent weighs his or her own needs versus those of the child versus those of the co-parent versus materialistic needs.

Family conflict, chaos and transition can induce guilt and prompt some parents to withdraw parenting limits and consequences, adding to the child's confusion and anxiety.

References

Ackerson, B. J. (2003) Coping with the dual demands of severe mental illness and parenting: the parents' perspective. *Family in Society*, 84, 109-118.

American Psychological Association. (APA; 2010). Guidelines for child custody evaluations in family law proceedings. *American Psychologist*, 65, 863-867.

Association of Family and Conciliation Courts. (AFCC; 2007). Model standards of practice for child custody evaluation. *Family Court Review*, 45(1), 70-91.

Behrens, K. Y. Hesse, E. Main, M. (2007). Mothers' attachment status as determined by the Adult Attachment Interview predicts their 6-year-olds' reunion responses: A study conducted in Japan. *Developmental Psychology*, 43(6), 1553-1567.

Chi, Liping. (2013). Intergenerational transmission of educational attainment: Three levels of parent–child communication as mediators. *PsyCh Journal*, 2(1), 26-38.

Conger, R.D. Schofield, T.J. Neppl, T.K. Merrick, M. (2013). Disrupting intergenerational continuity in harsh and abusive parenting: The importance of a nurturing relationship with a romantic partner. *J Adolesc Health*, 53(4 Suppl), S11-S17.

Creech, S. K. Hadley, W. Borsari, B. (2014). The impact of military deployment and reintegration on children and parenting: A systematic review. *Professional Psychology: Research and Practice*, 45, 452-464.

Finzi-Dottan, Ricky; Harel, Galit. (2014). Parents' potential for child abuse: An intergenerational perspective. *Journal of Family Violence*, 29(4), 397-408.

Friedman, Susan Hatters; Evans, Thomas M. (2006). Termination of parental rights. *Journal of the American Academy of Psychiatry and the Law*, 34(4), 551-553.

Garber, B. (2004). Parental alienation in light of attachment theory: Consideration of the broader implications for child development, clinical practice, and forensic process. *Journal of Child Custody*, 1(4), 49-76.

Garber, B. D. (2010). *Developmental psychology for family law professionals: Theory, application and the best interests of the child*. New York: Springer.

Garber, B. D. (2011). Parental alienation and the dynamics of the enmeshed parent-child dyad: Adultification, parentification, and infantilization. *Family Court Review*, 49, 322–335.

Gould, J. W. Martindale, D. A. (2007). *The art and science of child custody evaluations*. New York: Wiley.

Hynan, D. (2014). *Child Custody Evaluations*. Charles C. Thomas: Springfield, Illinois.

Itäpuisto, Maritta Sisko. (2014). Helping the children of substance-abusing parents in the context of outpatient substance abuse treatment. *Addiction Research & Theory*, 22(6), 498-504.

Jennings, Wesley G.; Park, MiRang; Richards, Tara N.; Tomsich, Elizabeth; Gover, Angela; Powers, Ráchael A. (2014). Exploring the relationship between child physical abuse and adult dating violence using a causal inference approach in an emerging adult population in South Korea. *Child Abuse & Neglect*, 38(12), 1902-1913.

Kachadourian, L.K. Eiden, R.D. Leonard, K.E. (2009). Paternal alcoholism, negative parenting, and the mediating role of marital satisfaction. *Addictive Behaviors*, 34, 918-927.

King, H. (2013). Assessment in custody hearings: Child custody evaluations. In K. F. Geisinger B. A. Bracken J. F. Carlson J. C. Hansen N. R. Kuncel S. P. Reise M. C. Rodriguez (Eds.) *APA handbook of testing and assessment in psychology, Vol. 2: Testing and assessment in clinical and counseling psychology* (pp. 587-605). Washington, DC: American Psychological Association.

Klahr, A. M. Burt, S. A. (2014). Elucidating the etiology of individual differences in parenting: A meta-analysis of behavior genetic research. *Psychological Bulletin*, 140, 544-586.

Merrick, M.T. Leeb, R.T. Lee, R.D. (2013). Examining the role of safe, stable, and nurturing relationships in the intergenerational continuity of child maltreatment—Introduction to the Special Issue. *J Adolesc Health*, 53(4 Suppl), S1-S3.

O'Donnell, Ellen H.; Eddy, Kamryn T.; Rauch, Paula K. (2013) In Heru, Alison M. (Ed), *Parenting with chronic and life-threatening illness: A parent guidance model. Working with families in medical settings: A multidisciplinary guide for psychiatrists and other health professionals*, (pp. 130-147). New York, NY, US: Routledge/Taylor & Francis Group.

Parade, S. H., Supple, A. J., & Helms, H. M. (2012). Parenting during childhood predicts relationship satisfaction in young adulthood: A prospective longitudinal perspective. *Marriage and Family Review*, 48, 150-169.

Parke, Ross D. (2013). Gender differences and similarities in parental behavior. In Wilcox, W. Bradford (Ed); Kovner Kline, Kathleen (Eds.), *Gender and parenthood: Biological and social scientific perspectives*, (pp. 120-163). New York, NY, US: Columbia University Press.

Pears, K.C. Kim, H.K. Capaldi, D. Kerr &, D.C. Fisher, P.A. (2013). Father-child transmission of school adjustment: a prospective intergenerational study. *Dev. Psychol.* 49, 792-803.

Roxburgh, Susan; Fitch, Chivon (2014). Parental status, child contact, and well-being among incarcerated men and women. *Journal of Family Issues*, 35(10), 1394-1412.

Schofield, T.J. Lee, R.D. Merrick, M.T. (2013). Safe, stable, nurturing relationships as a moderator of intergenerational continuity of child maltreatment: A meta-analysis. *J Adolesc Health*, 53(4 Suppl), S32-S38.

Stafström, Martin (2014). Influence of parental alcohol-related attitudes, behavior and parenting styles on alcohol use in late and very late adolescence. *European Addiction Research*, 20(5), 241-247.

Villalta, Laia; Arévalo, Rubén; Valdepérez, Ana; Pascual, Juan C.; los Cobos, J. Pérez (2014). Parental bonding in subjects with pathological gambling disorder compared with healthy controls. *Psychiatric Quarterly*, No Pagination Specified.

Yeo, Lay See; Ong, Winston W.; Ng, Charis M. (2014). The home literacy environment and preschool children's reading skills and interest. *Early Education and Development*, 25(6), 791-814.

C. Co-parenting

Rationale and Uses

It does take a village to raise a child, but the villagers need to be willing to cooperate, communicate and to establish consistent caregiving practices if the child is to be healthy. This is co-parenting: The proactive collaboration of two or more adults who share a responsibility to a child's well-being.

When co-parents work together as caregiving partners, putting aside their feelings regardless of their legal, genetic or cohabitation status, children feel supported. Secure. When co-parents allow their adult differences to compromise their mutual caregiving –when communication fails, cooperation ceases and decisions become more about self or harming the other than about serving the child's needs- children are harmed.

When the court orders that divorcing adults share decision-making authority for their child, it is requiring those adults to cooperate and to communicate. When co-parents are incapable of these basic, mature functions, shared decision making authority is little more than an invitation to stalemate and missed opportunities. Where Mom and Dad might negotiate summer camp or permission to go on a field trip, oboe lessons or driver's ed, conflict erupts instead.

Co-parenting capacity bears similarly on the determination of the child's schedule of care. Ordering a child to migrate between parents who hate one another several times each week risks placing the child in a war zone over and over again. On the other hand, co-parents who can communicate constructively may be able to make the child's transition from one to another benign. (Garber, 2009).

These same variables are relevant to therapists providing co-parent interventions (e.g., Garber, 2004) and to parenting coordinators (Deutsch, 2014). In both arenas, the professional is tasked to help parenting partners develop their capacity for child-centered communication, cooperation and consistency.

"The Co-parenting Questionnaire" was developed to serve all of these purposes: To help forensic evaluators assess critical facets of the co-parenting relationship as these may bear on the child's well-being and the future allocation of parenting rights and responsibilities, and to help those tasked with facilitating the co-parenting relationship better target goals for intervention and to track progress across time.

Co-Parenting Questionnaire
© 2006-2013 Benjamin D. Garber, Ph.D.

Please print your name:	What is your relationship to the child(ren):
	(examples: Mother? Father? Step-mother? Dad's girlfriend? Mom's partner? Grandmother? Aunt? Foster mother?)
Today's Date: _____	

A co-parent is any adult with whom you share responsibility for the care of one or more children, no matter that adult's emotional, biological or legal relationship to you or to the child. This questionnaire will help to understand the co-parenting relationship between you and one of your co-parents.

Please complete this questionnaire once about your relationship with each of your co-parents. For example, a father might complete this questionnaire once about his co-parenting relationship with his child(ren)'s mother and then complete a second copy of the same questionnaire time about his co-parenting relationship with the child's step-father.

The following answers are about your co-parenting relationship with:	This co-parent's relationship to the child(ren) is:
(please name the co-parent)	(examples: Mother? Father? Step-mother? Dad's girlfriend? Mom's partner? Grandmother? Aunt? Foster mother?)

What is the status of your relationship with this co-parent?	1 ___ Living together full time	2 ___ Never married
	___ Living together sometimes	___ Married
	___ Living apart full time	___ Divorcing or divorced

Mom and dad are divorced.

Dad is remarried.

Mom shares parenting responsibilities with her mom. Each parent should complete the form twice, once about the other biological parent, and once about their other parenting partner (step-mom for dad; grandma for mom).

What about step-mom and maternal grandma?

The value in asking them to complete this questionnaire and their role in the larger evaluation will depend on the question being addressed.

Who is a co-parent?

It is quite common for courts and attorneys and litigating parties to argue this question when, in fact, the child-centered answer is simple: Everyone who shares a responsibility to care for a specific child regardless of gender, generation or geography. If the child's needs are really the issue, then mom's resentment of dad's new girlfriend and dad's resistance to acknowledging mom's nanny won't matter. They all have valuable perspectives and they all need to be on the same page.

FORM 5: The Co-parenting Questionnaire
Page 2 of 2

This co-parent and I ...	Never				Always
1. Put our child(ren)'s needs first	0	1	2	3	4
2. Treat the child(ren) as friends	0	1	2	3	4
3. Understand what our child(ren) want and need	0	1	2	3	4
4. Argue about which of us is right	0	1	2	3	4
5. Stay in touch with the child(ren)'s teachers and doctors	0	1	2	3	4
6. Can not talk about the child(ren)	0	1	2	3	4

This co-parent and I ...	Never				Always
7. Communicate with one another about the child(ren)	0	1	2	3	4
8. Make plans for the child(ren) without informing each other	0	1	2	3	4
9. Know how to reach one another at all times	0	1	2	3	4
10. Ask the child(ren) to communicate adult information to their other parent	0	1	2	3	4
11. Routinely share information about our child(ren)	0	1	2	3	4
12. Keep secrets about the child(ren) from one another	0	1	2	3	4

This co-parent and I ...	Never				Always
13. Present a united front to the child(ren)	0	1	2	3	4
14. Have separate rules and limits for the child(ren)	0	1	2	3	4
15. Support one another's parenting decisions	0	1	2	3	4
16. Approach parenting differently	0	1	2	3	4
17. Follow through with the other parent's decisions for the child(ren)	0	1	2	3	4
18. Ignore or disregard each other's parenting decisions	0	1	2	3	4

This co-parent and I ...	Never				Always
19. Speak positively about one another to the child(ren)	0	1	2	3	4
20. Ask the child(ren) to choose between us	0	1	2	3	4
21. Respect each other as parents	0	1	2	3	4
22. Ask the child(ren) to keep secrets from their other parent	0	1	2	3	4
23. Know that the child(ren) are well cared-for with the other parent	0	1	2	3	
24. Insult or curse one another around the child(ren)	0	1	2	3	4

Child-centeredness:

Boundaries and limits; putting the children's needs first

Communication:

How and when and with what media do the adults update one another and address concerns?

(e.g., Bowers et al., 2014 and check out online resources such as www.OurFamilyWizard.com).

Consistency of parenting practices:

How similar or different are the expectations, rules, consequences and rituals between the homes?

Mutual alignment:

Does each parent support the child's opportunity to maintain a healthy relationship with all others?

Read about the "friendly parent doctrine"

(e.g., Warshak, 2015).

A special case:

How does a child's chronic illness impact co-parenting?
(see McNeil et al., 2014)

FORM 5: The Co-parenting Questionnaire Scoring Protocol

1. **There are four categories:**
   (a) Child-centeredness
   (b) Communication
   (c) Consistency
   (d) Mutual alignment

2. **Each category contains six items.**
   (a) Non-shaded items are scored based on their face value, that is, if the number 3 is circled, this is scored = 3.
   (b) Responses to shaded items are reversed, that is the face value is subtracted from 4. Thus, if the number 3 is circled, 4-3 = 1. This is scored = 1.
   (c) Responses between numbers must be clarified.

3. All six scored responses within each category are summed to create a score from 0 to 24. This yields four category sums per respondent, one for each of the four categories.

4. Differences and similarities in responses can be compared between respondents at a single time and/or within respondents over time.

References

Abidin, R. and Brunner, J. (1995). Development of a parenting alliance inventory. *Journal of Clinical Child Psychology*, 24, 31-40.

Altenburger, Lauren E.; Schoppe-Sullivan, Sarah J.; Lang, Sarah N.; Bower, Daniel J.; Kamp Dush, Claire M. (2014). Associations between prenatal coparenting behavior and observed coparenting. *Journal of Family Psychology*, 28(4), Aug 495-504.

Attorney General of Texas. (2010). For Our Children: A Co-parenting Guide. Available online at https://texasattorneygeneral.gov/files/cs/coparenting.pdf

Baum, N. (2003). Divorce process variables and the co-parental relationship and parental role fulfillment of divorced parents. *Family Process*, 42(1), 117-131

Bowers, Jill R.; Ogolsky, Brian G.; Hughes Jr., Robert; Kanter, Jeremy B. (2014). Coparenting through divorce or separation: A review of an online program. *Journal of Divorce & Remarriage,* 55(6), 464-484.

Brody, G. and Flor, D. (1996). Co-parenting, family interactions, and competence among African American youths. In J.P.McHale & P.A. Cowan (eds.), *New directions for child development. Volume 74: Understanding how family-level dynamics affect children's development: Studies of two-parent families.* San Francisco: Jossey-Bass.

Deutsch, Robin M. (2014). Parenting coordination: Basic approaches and strategies. In Higuchi, Shirley Ann & Lally, Stephen J. (Eds.), *Parenting coordination in postseparation disputes: A comprehensive guide for practitioners.* , (pp. 63-74). Washington, DC, US: American Psychological Association.

Finzi-Dottan, R. Cohen, O. (2014). Predictors of parental communication and cooperation among divorcing Spouses. *Journal of Child and Family Studies*, 23, 39-41.

Garber, B. (2004). Directed Coparenting Intervention: Conducting child-centered interventions in parallel with highly conflicted co-parents. *Professional Psychology, Research and Practice*, 35, 55-64. doi:10.1037/0735-7028.35.1.55

Garber, B. (2004). Parental alienation in light of attachment theory: Consideration of the broader implications for child development, clinical practice, and forensic process. *Journal of Child Custody*, 1(4), 49-76.

Garber, B. D. (2010). *Developmental psychology for family law professionals: Theory, application and the best interests of the child*. New York: Springer.

Grych, J. and Fincham, F. (2001). *Child development and interparental conflict*. NY: Cambridge University Press.

Kerig, P. (1998). Moderators and mediators of the effects of interparental conflict on children's adjustment. *Journal of Abnormal Child Psychology*, 26, 199-212.

Massachusetts Chapter of the Association of Family and Conciliation Courts. (2010). *Planning for Shared Parenting: A Guide For Parents living Apart.* Available online at:http://www.masslegalhelp.org/children-and-families/afcc-shared-parenting-planning.pdf.

McConnell, M. and Kerig, P. (2002). Assessing co-parenting in families of school-age children: Validation of the Co-parenting and Family Rating System. *Canadian Journal of Behavioural Science*, 34(1), 44-58.

McNeill, Ted; Nicholas, David; Beaton, John; Montgomery, Gert; MacCulloch, Radha; Gearing, Robin; Selkirk, Enid (2014). The coconstruction of couples' roles in parenting children with a chronic health condition. *Qualitative Health Research*, 24(8), 1114-1125.

Thayer, E. and Zimmerman, J. (2001). *The Co-Parenting Survival Guide*. Oakland, CA: New Harbinger.

Warshak, R. (2015). Securing children's best interests while avoiding the lure of simple solutions. *Journal of Divorce & Remarriage*, 56: 57-79

D. Child Development

Rationale and Uses

A child's developmental status is at least as important to family law decisions as it is misunderstood. Across jurisdictions and areas of jurisprudence, child-centered outcomes are determined in part based on metrics mistaken for development such as age or maturity. We all know, for example, that children cannot vote or drive or purchase alcohol before they have lived a predetermined and somewhat random number of years.

English Common Law referred to the "rule of sevens:" Children were deemed incompetent to make decisions from birth until age 7, worth listening to from age 7 to fourteen, and accountable for their choices after age fourteen. This (empirically unsupported) standard has been inherited in many jurisdictions today as a 'mature minor' statute, granting children ages fourteen and older the opportunity to be heard in matters concerning their well-being.[7]

Child-centered forensic evaluators are responsible to understand the child's developmental course, a process best understood as beginning at or even before conception. This includes obtaining caregiver's reports of the child's physical, social, emotional and academic growth. The "**Child's Developmental History**" questionnaire helps to collect and organize these data in advance of interview and for comparison with pediatric, academic and related third party objective accounts.

---

[7] This is a huge subject and far beyond the scope of these pages. In very short form, the reader is directed to my discussion of the mature minor concept in Garber (2010) and to the United Nations Convention on The Rights of the Child available online at: http://www.ohchr.org/en/professionalinterest/pages/crc.aspx.

Child's Developmental History
© 1990-2015 Benjamin D. Garber, Ph.D.

Caregivers: This questionnaire requests information about a specific child's history of growth and development from conception through the present. Your assistance providing accurate information will be very helpful. Please take the time to complete all relevant pages as thoroughly as possible. Feel free to add any additional comments or observations on the reverse of any page. Thank you, in advance, for completing this questionnaire

Please note that a separate questionnaire must be completed about each child.

Who is completing this questionnaire: _____
(please print your name and relationship to the child)

A. Demographics:

1. This child's full name is: _____

2. This child's date of birth is: _____ (mo/date/yr)

3. As of (date present schedule began) _____ this child resides at:

Street address of the residence	What days/times does this child reside at this address?

4. This child is presently in _____ grade and attends (please name school and address):

_____

5. How would you describe this child's physical appearance (attach a recent photo if possible):

_____

6. Please describe on the reverse how the child understands the family's current situation (e.g., the ., how the child understands change, loss, parental separation, divorce, adoption)

The child-centered forensic evaluator should always ask adults what the child has been told about the family situation (e.g., divorce) and what the child understands.

When the evaluator plans to meet the child, it is often important to explicitly script how the parents should describe the evaluator's role to the children.

All of the questionnaires discussed in this volume are intended to be printed on one side of the page only.

Respondents are invited to elaborate on any item the reverse side.

Child's name: _____   Page 2

B. In general about this child:

7. Has this child....?   Please explain any
                                                             YES responses on the reverse

a.	...had any prolonged absences from school?	☐ yes
b.	...failed or repeated a grade?	☐ yes
c.	...had psychological testing, counseling or psychotherapy of any kind?	☐ yes
d.	...had speech/language, O.T., P.T., or audiological testing or treatment?	☐ yes
e.	...been suspended or expelled from any activity or institution?	☐ yes
f.	...been involved with police or any legal matter?	☐ yes
g.	...run away from home or school or threatened to do so?	☐ yes
h.	...talked about, planned or acted to intentionally harm him- or herself?	☐ yes
i.	...talked about, planned or acted to intentionally harm, other people?	☐ yes
j.	...experimented with, used or become dependent on any substance?	☐ yes
k.	...been neglected, abused, molested or otherwise traumatized?	☐ yes
l.	...expressed concern about the family (e.g., a wish to live with others or elsewhere?)	☐ yes
m.	...been exposed to (but not the victim of) violence?	☐ yes
n.	...had any serious illness, injury or surgery?	☐ yes
o.	...been on any prescription medication?	☐ yes
p.	...had difficulties with anxiety, worry or fears?	☐ yes
q.	...been uncharacteristically irritable or explosive, withdrawn or unresponsive?	☐ yes
r.	...been suspected of having or diagnosed as having a learning or attention difficulty?	☐ yes
s.	...been exposed to any adult's words or actions damning one or both parents?	☐ yes
t.	...blamed him- or herself for family problems?	☐ yes
u.	...had difficulties with eating, sleeping or toileting?	☐ yes
v.	...reported seeing, hearing or otherwise sensing things that were not there?	☐ yes
w.	...had difficulty making or maintaining friendships?	☐ yes
x.	...been bullied or rejected?	☐ yes
y.	...have odd habits or rituals, beliefs or practices?	☐ yes

No checklist can be exhaustive, but I find that YES responses on this page are an excellent guide to what to ask in subsequent interview and what relevant documentation to request.

Do Mom and Dad respond YES to the same items?

Are differences due to oversight, obfuscation or ignorance?

Can you access objective records documenting areas of concern:

School testing? Police records?

Hospital reports? Psychotherapy records?

FORM 6: Child's Developmental History
Page 3 of 12

Child's name: _____   Page 3

C. Conception and delivery:

8. This child is adopted   ☐ yes ☐ no

    If **YES**, please describe what is known about the child's biological parents and the circumstances of adoption on the reverse

9. Was this child's conception planned?   ☐ yes ☐ no

10. How long was necessary to become pregnant?   _____ months

11. What was the father's reaction upon learning of The pregnancy?

12. What was the mother's reaction upon learning of The pregnancy?

13. Was the baby carried full term (9 months)?   ☐ yes ☐ no

14. At birth the child weighed (pounds and ounces)?

15. At birth the child was how long (inches)?

16. During pregnancy, the mother...

    ☐ Smoked tobacco   ☐ Drank alcohol
    ☐ Was injured, fell or in an accident   ☐ Had a serious illness or surgery
    ☐ Used prescription medications
      (please specify): _____
    ☐ Experienced other major stress
      (please specify): _____

17. Describe the child's delivery...

    ☐ Vaginal, uneventful and healthy   ☐ Cesarean section and healthy
    ☐ V-back (second or subsequent birth)   ☐ Mother had general anesthetic
    ☐ Mother and child had skin to skin contact immediately or shortly after delivery
    ☐ Baby experienced fetal distress (please specify on the reverse)
    ☐ Father held the baby within the first hours after delivery
    ☐ Mother had medical event that complicated delivery

18. The child's APGAR scores at birth were: _____ and _____

19. Mother returned home _____ days after delivery

20. Child returned home _____ days after delivery

Infertility is a very powerful marital and family stressor that is often overlooked

(e.g., Onat & Beji, 2012)

Premature, ill and failure to thrive infants are both important family stressors and can be predictors of later health and academic difficulties

(e.g., Howe et al., 2014).

Read more here about mother-child and father-child perinatal skin-to-skin contact:

(Rutgers & Myers, 2014), and in particular the benefits to preemies (e.g., Feldman et al., 2014).

Did the premature infant have frequent contact with his or her parents even while in hospital?

(e.g., Flacking et al., 2012)

Perinatal bonding experiences vary by culture but are often associated with greater parental warmth and later secure attachments

(e.g., Brockington, 2008).

FORM 6: Child's Developmental History
Page 4 of 12

D.   Infancy and toddler years
(approximately ages birth through 2 years old)

21. Please use this table to indicate who was PRIMARILY responsible for each activity during the child's first two years:

	Mother:	Father:	Both Mother and Father:	Other Caregiver (please identify)
Feeding:				
Bathing:				
Diapering:				
Responding to distress:				
Playing:				
Meeting other children:				

22. During the first two years of life, please indicate who or what helped to calm this child? (Check all that are true)

☐	Mother's pick-up, proximity or voice	☐	Bottle or breast
☐	Father's pick-up, proximity or voice	☐	Pacifier
☐	Another caregiver's pick-up, proximity or voice	☐	Special object ("blankie" or stuffed animal)
☐	No one was able to calm this child when distressed	☐	Nothing helped to calm this child when distressed

23. Was this child breast fed?   ☑ yes   ☐ no

If YES, what ages? _____

24. Did you feel that any of this child's early behavior was odd or unusual?   ☐ yes   ☐ no

If YES, please specify on the reverse

25. Please note the approximate ages at which each of the following developmental milestones occurred:

Behavior	Months old	Behavior	Months old
Sits unassisted		Stands unassisted	
Says first real words		Walks unassisted	
Says first sentences		Clean and dry days	
Sleeps through the night		Clean and dry overnight	
First experienced conflict in the home		Fears strangers	
First separation from either parent		Clingy, separation anxiety	

Custody-related matters often ask who is/was the child's primary caregiver?

Parents seldom agree.

(See Warshak, 2015 re: "the approximation rule")

Breast-feeding practices and attitudes vary by culture (e.g., Street & Lewallen, 2013)

Nursing can be associated with postpartum depression (e.g., Dias & Figueiredo, 2014)

Child's name: _____   Page 5

26. What three adjectives best describe the child during his or her first two years?

_____, _____, _____

28. What was the most difficult part of this child's first two years?

29. Did this child experience a prolonged or traumatic separation from any caregiver during the first two years? If YES, please explain on reverse   ☑ yes   ☐ no

30. Did the child have any other caregivers in his or her life during the first two years (examples: grandparents, babysitters, nannies) If YES please identify on reverse   ☐ yes   ☑ no

I have found that soliciting adjectives from respondents can provide powerful insights in many different contexts.

"Prolonged" and "traumatic" are intentionally subjective terms.

Extended infant-caregiver separations can be associated with depression, regression and developmental delay in children and depression in adults.

"…the occurrence of a mother-child separation of a week or longer within the first two years of life was related to higher levels of child negativity (at age 3) and aggression (at ages 3 and 5)"

Parent-child separation (see Rutter, 1971 for a general overview) has often been examined in the context of incarceration (e.g., Schlager & Moore, 2014), hospitalization (e.g., Howard et al., 2012) and military deployment (e.g., Creech et al., 2014; Faber et al., 2008), but little is known about the developmental impact of the separations associated with shared parenting schedules (e.g., see Schen, 2005).

Child's name: _____   Page 6

E. Preschool Years
(approximately ages 2 to 5 years old)

31. Please use this table to indicate how this child responds/responded to specific caregivers and situations during the 2 to 5 year old preschool period

	Happy	Indifferent	Upset	This situation never occurred
Approached by mother				
Held by mother				
Plays near mother				
Separated from mother				
Approached by father				
Held by father				
Plays near father				
Separated from father				
Approached by stranger				
Held by stranger				
Plays near stranger				
Separated from stranger				
Approached by another child or sibling				
Plays near another child or sibling				
Separated from another child or sibling				

32. Did/does this child have/had a favorite object (toy, blanket, stuffed animal?) which seemed to comfort him or her when distressed? If YES, when did the child give this object up?   ☑ yes   ☐ no

_____ months old

33. How often did/does this child spend time with other 2-5 year olds during this period:

☐ Rarely or never	☐ sometimes	☐ Often
☑ Participated in playgroup	☐ Attended daycare or preschool	☐ Frequent informal playdates

33. This child's favorite playmates during this period are/were:

_____ , _____

How a child learns to calm him- or herself is the beginning of self-regulation. These questions ask about who and what soothes the preschool-aged child.

Explore how parents understand and support the child's use of transitional objects e.g., in the context of foster care and adoption (Fallon & Goldsmith, 2013). Parent anxiety mediates peer competence.

Parent anxiety mediates preschoolers' peer competence (e.g., Wichstrøm et al., 2013)

Whether infants and preschoolers should have over-nights when parents live apart has been a highly controversial issue for years.

Read recent positions on this question:

(e.g., Neilsen, 2014; Warshak, 2000; Cashmere et al., 2008; Garber, 2012)

Child's name: _____ Page 7

34. Please note the approximate ages at which each of the following developmental milestones occurred:

Behavior	Months old	Behavior	Months old
Ties shoes		Dresses unassisted	
Cleans up when asked		Brushes own teeth	
Birth of next sibling		Clean and dry days and nights	
Began preschool or daycare		Toilets unassisted	
Introduction of new caregiver in the home		Comfortable with transitions and change	
Fell asleep in his her own bed alone		Shares and cooperates with peers	

35. Please describe the rules, rewards or punishments routinely used with this child during the 2-5 year old period:

Rule or expectation:	Compliance earns what reward or punishment:	Non-compliance earns what punishment or consequence:
Example: Put away toys	Earn allowance	Toys are taken away
a.		
b.		
c.		
d.		

Among these indices, the child's opportunity and willingness to fall asleep in bed alone speaks to self-regulation and emotional maturity

How much structure do parents have?

Are expectations clear and follow-through consistent? Are successes rewarded or do parents wait to punish failure?

Read Baumrind (2013) about **authoritative parenting.**

FORM 6: Child's Developmental History
Page 8 of 12

Child's name: _____   Page 8

F. Elementary School Years
(approximately ages 6 to 11 years old)

36. This child attends/attended:
☐ Public school   ☐ Private school   ☐ Parochial school   ☐ Home schooling

37. This child's grades are/were:
☐ A-B   ☐ B-C   ☐ C-D   ☐ Highly variable

38. This child receives/received special education services   ☐ yes   ☐ no
    If YES, please explain on the reverse side

39. This child's FAVORITE subject in school is/was:

40. This child's BEST subject in school is/was:

41. This child's WORST subject in school is/was:

42. What three adjectives best describe the child during this period?

43. This child's social experience during this period is best described as:

☐ A loner, uninvolved   ☐ Interested but isolated; on   ☐ Involved with a small
                                    the edges   group
☐ Accepted and involved   ☐ Popular, even distracted by   ☐ Bullied, harassed and
                                    relationships   rejected

44. Please indicate what EXTRA-CURRICULAR or CO-CURRICULAR activities this child participates/participated in during elementary school. Continue on the reverse if necessary.

Activity	Ages participated	Enjoyed participating?	Successful participant?

45. In elementary school, this child wants/wanted to be what as an adult:

Children's academic performance is often a barometer of emotional distress.

Extracurricular involvement is associated with academic achievement (e.g. Seow et al., 2014)

But extracurriculars are often the first loss when families are in conflict.

FORM 6: Child's Developmental History
Page 9 of 12

Child's name: _____   Page 9

G.   Junior High and High School Years
(approximately ages 12 to 18 years old)

46. This child attends/attended:
☐ Public school   ☐ Private school   ☐ Parochial school   ☐ Home schooling

47. Please use the conventional A=excellent, B=very good, C=average, D=passing and F=failure grades to describe the child's academic performance in these years:

____ Math   ____ Science   ____ Reading   ____ Music/Art

____ English   ____ Social Studies   ____ Foreign   ____ Physical
                                               language   education

48. Has this child ever been disciplined in school for behavior problems?   ☐ yes   ☐ no
    If YES, please explain on the reverse side

49. This child receives/received special education services   ☑ yes   ☐ no
    If YES, please explain on the reverse side

50. What three adjectives best describe the child during this period?

_____, _____, _____

51. This child's social experience during this period is best described as:

☐ A loner, uninvolved   ☐ Interested but isolated; on   ☐ Involved with a small
                                   the edges   group
☐ Accepted and involved   ☐ Popular, even distracted by   ☐ Bullied, harassed and
                                   relationships   rejected

52. Please indicate what EXTRA-CURRICULAR or CO-CURRICULAR activities this child participates/participated in during elementary school. Continue on the reverse if necessary.

Activity	Ages participated	Enjoyed participating?	Successful participant?

53. In junior high and high school, this child wants/wanted to be what as an adult:

_____

Get a copy of the IEP or 504 plan. The nature of the child's needs will be relevant and so, too, will be the sense of which parent(s) are participating in the process.

Is the child expressing an interest in being more like one parent than the other? What might this mean for relationships in the family?

Regarding gender identification and career aspirations see e.g., Pizzorno, 2014

FORM 6: Child's Developmental History
Page 10 of 12

H.   Maturity and Responsibility

54. Please note the approximate ages at which each of the following developmental milestones occurred:

Milestone achieved	Child's age	Milestone achieved	Child's age
Learned the names of male and female genitalia ("private parts")		Understood "where babies come from" (intercourse; procreation)	
Shows interest in sexuality (e.g., pornography)		Acting out in a sexualized manner	
Began dating		Have first girlfriend or boyfriend	
Became sexually active with a partner		Body began puberty	
Began using birth control methods		Body completed puberty	
Exposed to sexual behavior of others		Sexually molested, abused or mistreated in any way	

55. In the present, is this child presently mature and responsible? ☐ yes ☐ no
56. Does this child reliably complete chores at home when asked? ☐ yes ☐ no
57. Does this child complete homework independently? ☐ yes ☐ no
58. Is this child responsible with his or her possessions (e.g., toys, electronics, clothes, school materials)? ☐ yes ☐ no
59. Has this child ever had a job or any sort? ☐ yes ☐ no
60. Does this child treat pets and other animals responsibly? ☐ yes ☐ no
61. Does this child care for him- or herself (bathing, brushing teeth, haircare)? ☐ yes ☐ no
62. Is this child responsible about getting to bed on time? ☐ yes ☐ no
63. Is this child responsible about waking up for school? ☐ yes ☐ no
64. Is this child responsible with curfew? ☐ yes ☐ no
65. Has this child begun driving at all? ☐ yes ☐ no
66. If so, is this child a responsible and safe driver? ☐ yes ☐ no

67. Please describe what the child does when experiencing each of the following:

Happy:	
Sad:	
Mad:	
Scared:	

A history of alleged or founded sexual abuse must be thoroughly explored

(e.g., Kuehnle & Connell, 2013, 2010 and Williams et al., 2014)

Beware that "maturity" is not a singular development like height or weight.

We each mature in different domains at different rates so that a child's social, emotional, moral and physical maturity can be quite different.

Children triangulated into adult conflict can develop a very impressive façade of social maturity that hides neediness and upset.

Don't be fooled by a child who can look you in the eye and say all the right things – parents often are. Read more about the "chameleon child" (Garber, 2014)

Child's name: _____   Page 11

I.   Medical

Has this child ever...? Please elaborate on all YES responses on the reverse

68.	Required surgery of any kind?	☐ yes	☐ no
69.	Required hospitalization at any time?	☐ yes	☐ no
70.	Had a head injury?	☐ yes	☐ no
71.	Been diagnosed with a chronic or serious illness?	☐ yes	☐ no
72.	Lost consciousness, had a seizure or "black out"?	☐ yes	☐ no

73. **Please list this child's present medications and dietary supplements below:**

Name of medication/supplement	dosage	Prescribed by whom?	Reason for medication

74. **Please list this child's present physical health concerns, dietary limitations or restrictions:**

Nature of limitations or restriction	Reason

75. Are this child's immunizations up to date?   ☐ yes   ☐ no

76. Please identify any chronic or serious physical or mental illness among people related to this child:

Relation to child (e.g., maternal grandfather)	Illness

It's often necessary and appropriate to obtain medical records.

Beware that HIPAA laws will be a hurdle (e.g., Schlam & Wood, 2000).

Some institutions will insist that their proprietary consents are signed and will not accept yours.

Understand parenting a sick child (e.g., Carter, 2014).

A child's chronic illness can increase the risk of abuse (e.g., Svensson et al., 2013).

Chronic illness can affect developmental progress (e.g., Pinquart, 2014) and has demonstrable impact on the co-parenting relationship (e.g., Mednick & Koocher, 2014).

FORM 6: Child's Developmental History
Page 12 of 12

Child's name: _____

J.   In And Around The Child's Home(s)

77. I reside in:
- ☐ Single family home
- ☐ Apartment with two or more bedrooms
- ☐ Apartment with one bedroom
- ☐ Duplex
- ☐ House trailer
- ☐ Other: _____

78. My home is:
- ☐ In a rural setting
- ☐ In a suburban setting
- ☐ In an urban (city) setting
- ☐ Walking distance from the child's school
- ☐ 10-minutes or less by car to the child's school
- ☐ More than a 10-minute car ride to school
- ☐ Near groceries and shopping
- ☐ Near the child's friends' homes
- ☐ Near the child's other parent's home

79. When the child lives in my home, which of the following are true (check all that apply):
- ☐ Child has his/her own room
- ☐ Child has his/her own bed
- ☐ Child has his/her own bathroom
- ☐ Child has access to a safe yard/play area outdoors
- ☐ Child has friends nearby
- ☐ Child has access to phone, TV/ computer

80. The child resides in my home at all times   ☐ yes   ☐ no
   If YES, please skip the next question

81. The child resides in my home (indicate times that the child is typically in your residential care on a two week schedule. This schedule does not include holidays and vacations):

		Sunday	Monday	Tuesday	Wednesday	Thursday	Friday	Saturday
WK1	a.m.							
	p.m.							
WK2	a.m.							
	p.m.							

82. I believe that the STRENGTHS of this home for the child are:
_____

83. I believe that the WEAKNESSES of this home for the child are:
_____

End of questionnaire. Thank you.

Children who migrate between caregivers spend a great deal of time in transit.

How do they experience this?

Do parents use this time as a "captive audience" opportunity to talk or distract the child with mobile devices?

Home visits can be a critical part of a forensic family evaluation (e.g., Saini & Polak, 2014).

If the respondent scratched and erased and then attached the court order while trying to describe the schedule of care on the calendar, above, or if you find it confusing, imagine how the child feels.

How many transitions between caregivers does the child make in each two-week period?

How many consecutive nights is the child apart from each parent in the same period?

In order to begin to understand the child's experience, balance these factors against how similar or disparate the parents' caregiving is and how much anxiety the child experiences at transition.

References

Baumrind, D. (2013). Authoritative parenting revisited: History and current status. In R. E. Larzelere A. Morris A. W. Harrist (Eds.), *Authoritative parenting: Synthesizing nurturance and discipline for optimal child development* (pp. 11-34). Washington, DC: American Psychological Association.

Brockington, Ian (2008). Maternal attachment and bonding disorders. In Stone, Susan Dowd & Menken, Alexis E. (Eds.), *Perinatal and postpartum mood disorders: Perspectives and treatment guide for the health care practitioner.* (pp. 17-39). New York, NY, US: Springer Publishing Co.

Carter, Bernie (2014). Parenting a sick child: Challenge and resilience. *Journal of Child Health Care*, 18(2), 99-100.

Cashmore, J. Parkinson, P. Taylor, A. (2008). Overnight stays and children's relationships with parents after divorce. *Journal of Family Issues*, 29, 707-733.

Creech, S. K. Hadley, W. Borsari, B. (2014). The impact of military deployment and reintegration on children and parenting: A systematic review. *Professional Psychology: Research and Practice*, 45, 452-464.

Dias, Cláudia Castro; Figueiredo, Bárbara (2014). Breastfeeding and depression: A systematic review of the literature. *Journal of Affective Disorders*, 171, 142-154.

Faber, A. J., Willerton, E., Clymer, S. R., MacDermid, S. M., & Weiss, H. M. (2008). Ambiguous absence, ambiguous presence: A qualitative study of military reserve families in wartime. *Journal of Family Psychology*, 22, 222–230.

Fallon, April E.; Goldsmith, Barbara L. (2013). Theoretical contributions to the understanding of parent-child bonding in adoption. In Brabender, Virginia M &. Fallon, April E. (Eds.), *Working with adoptive parents: Research, theory, and therapeutic interventions.* (pp. 23-44). Hoboken, NJ, US: John Wiley & Sons Inc,

Feldman, R. Rosenthal, Z. Eidelman, A.I. (2014). Maternal-preterm skin-to-skin contact enhances child physiologic organization and cognitive control across the first 10 years of life. *Biol Psychiatry*, 75(1), 56-64.

Flacking, R. Lehtonen, L. Thomson, G. Axelin, A. Ahlqvist, S. Moran, V. H. (2012). Closeness and separation in neonatal intensive care. *Acta Paediatr* 2012;101:1032-7

Garber, Benjamin D. (2010). *Developmental psychology for family law professionals: Theory, application and the best interests of the child.* New York: Springer.

Garber, Benjamin D. (2012). Security by association? Mapping attachment theory onto family law practice. *Family Court Review*, 50(3), 467-470.

Garber, Benjamin D. (2014). The chameleon child: Children as actors in the high conflict divorce drama. *Journal of Child Custody*, 11(1), 1-16.

Howard, K. Martin, A., Berlin, & Brooks-Gunn. (2011). Early mother-child separation, parenting, and child well-being in Early Head Start families. *Attachment & Human Development*, 13(1), 5-26.

Howe, Tsu-Hsin; Sheu, Ching-Fan; Wang, Tien-Ni; Hsu, Yung-Wen (2014). Parenting stress in families with very low birth weight preterm infants in early infancy. *Research in Developmental Disabilities*, 35(7), 1748-1756.

Kuehnle, K. Connell, M. (2010). Child sexual abuse suspicions: Treatment considerations during investigation. *Journal of Child Sexual Abuse*, 19, 554-571.

Kuehnle, Kathryn & Connell, Mary (2013). Child sexual abuse evaluations. In Otto, Randy K. & Weiner, Irving B. (Eds.), *Handbook of psychology, Vol. 11: Forensic psychology (2nd ed.).* , (pp. 579-613). Hoboken, NJ, US: John Wiley & Sons Inc,

Mednick, Lauren & Koocher, Gerald P. (2012). Co-parenting children with chronic medical conditions. In Kuehnle, Kathryn & Drozd, Leslie (Eds.), *Parenting plan evaluations: Applied research for the family court* (pp. 247-269). New York, NY, US: Oxford University Press.,

Nielsen, Linda (2014). Parenting plans for infants, toddlers, and preschoolers: Research and issues. *Journal of Divorce & Remarriage*, Vol 55(4), May 2014, 315-333.

Onat, G. & Beji, N. K. (2012). Marital relationship and quality of life among couples with infertility. *Sexuality and Disability*, 30(1), 39-52.

Pinquart, Martin (2014). Achievement of developmental milestones in emerging and young adults with and without pediatric chronic illness—A meta-analysis. *Journal of Pediatric Psychology*, 39(6), 577-587.

Pizzorno, Maria Chiara; Benozzo, Angelo; Fina, Alice; Sabato, Simonetta; Scopesi, Matteo (2014). Parent–child career construction: A narrative study from a gender perspective. *Journal of Vocational Behavior*, 84(3), 420-430.

Porche, Michelle V.; Sabalauskas, Kara; Ferreira, Heidi; Porche, Michelle V.; Sabalauskas, Kara; Ferreira, Heidi (2014). *Trauma and Mental Health As Barriers to Learning and Achievement for Youth in Residential Educational Settings.* American Psychological Association.

Rutgers, Suzanne Greydanus & Meyers, Sheryl (2014). Mother and newborn skin-to-skin contact. In Greydanus, Donald E., Feinberg, Arthur N., & Merrick, Joav

(Eds.), *Caring for the newborn: A comprehensive guide for the clinician. Pediatrics, child and adolescent health.* (pp. 87-94). Hauppauge, NY, US: Nova Biomedical Books.

Rutter, M. (1974). Parent-child separation: Psychological effects of children. *Psychiatrie de l'Enfant*, 17(2): 479-514.

Saini, Michael & Polak, Shely (2014). The ecological validity of parent-child observations: A review of empirical evidence related to custody evaluations. *Journal of Child Custody: Research, Issues, and Practices,* 11(3), 181-201.

Schlager, Melinda D. & Moore, Brenda (2014). Risk and resiliency of incarcerated mothers. *Families in Society*, 95(2), 100-106.

Schlam, L., & Wood, J. P. (2000). Informed consent to the medical treatment of minors: Law and practice. Health Matrix: *Journal of Law-Medicine*, 10, 141-174.

Seow, Poh-Sun & Pan, Gary (2014). A literature review of the impact of extracurricular activities participation on students' academic performance. *Journal of Education for Business*, 89(7), 361-366.

Street, D. J. Lewallen, L. P. (2013). The influence of culture on breast-feeding decisions by African American and white women. *Journal of Perinatal & Neonatal Nursing*, 27, 43-51.

Svensson, B. Eriksson, U. B. Janson, S. (2013). Exploring risk for abuse of children with chronic conditions or disabilities—parent's perceptions of stressors and the role of professionals. *Child Care Health Dev* 2013; 39:887-93.

Warshak, R. A. (2000). Blanket restrictions: Overnight contact between parents and young children. *Family and Conciliation Courts Review*, 38, 422-445.

Warshak, R. (2015). Securing children's best interests while avoiding the lure of simple solutions. *Journal of Divorce & Remarriage*, 56: 57-79

Wichstrøm, L. Belsky, J. Berg-Nielsen, T. S. (2013). Preschool predictors of childhood anxiety disorders: a prospective community study. *J Child Psychol Psychiatry*. 2013; 54(12): 1327-1336.

Williams, Javonda; Nelson-Gardell, Debra; Faller, Kathleen Coulborn; Tishelman, Amy & Cordisco-Steele, Linda (2014). Is there a place for extended assessments in addressing child sexual abuse allegations? How sensitivity and specificity impact professional perspectives. *Journal of Child Sexual Abuse: Research, Treatment, & Program Innovations for Victims, Survivors, & Offenders*, 23(2), 179-197

E. Parenting Capacity and Competence

Rationale and uses

Parenting capacity and competence are at the foundation of many forensic family evaluations (e.g., Choate & Engstrom, 2014; Pezzot-Pearce & Pearce, 2004). These essential skills underlie but not be mistaken for the questions of parent-child "fit" that arise in custody, visitation, placement, relocation and abuse/neglect matters.

Parenting capacity and competence evaluations ask generic, threshold questions about an adult's essential caregiving attitudes, beliefs and practices. What does he or she know about child and family development, behavior management and caregiving, in general? As such, parenting capacity and competence evaluations are *not* specific to any particular child and are not sufficient if the question before the court concerns a particular child's future care.

The available empirical data cataloguing types of parenting approaches and their respective impact on children's feelings, behavior and development is sound and impressive. Much of it rests on Baumrind's (1991, 2013) typology. She distinguishes between authoritative, authoritarian, permissive and disengaged parenting. Although the meaning and value of these types may differ to some degree by culture and circumstance (e.g., Uji et al., 2014; Watabe & Hibbard, 2014), authoritative parenting proves time and again to be associated with the healthiest outcomes.

I note that a current and comprehensive review finds very few reliable and valid measures of parenting capacity and competence (Hurley et al., 2014). **"The Parenting Stress Index"** (Abidin et al., 2006) being one notable exception.

Two instruments are introduced here. The reader is reminded that none of the resources provided herein has established psychometric properties. Each is intended to facilitate and standardize data collection largely to help the evaluator direct further inquiry.

The "**Semi-structured parenting capacity interview**" is precisely that: A roadmap with which an evaluator can elicit a range of factors relevant to parenting safety and an adult's attitudes and beliefs regarding variable related to the authoritative-authoritarian-permissive-disengaged typology. The instrument begins by examining each of eight parenting risk factors, each of which has an empirical basis discussed here. Responses to the subsequent eight typology questions allow an interviewer to hypothesize about where the respondent falls in Baumrind's typology.

"**Parenting Capacity Semi-Structured Interview / Parenting Capacity Questionnaire**" is a self-report questionnaire-style means of accessing similar information for a different purpose. By administering this instrument to two or more caregivers who share an interest in the well-being of a particular child, similarities and differences can be highlighted for subsequent exploration. Fifty true-false questions elicit adults' attitudes about the nine categories surveyed in the Semi-Structured Questionnaire. These are followed by a priorities ranking task very similar to the final page of the "**Individual Caregiver Personal and Parenting History**" (see page 27). This final page can be omitted if both instruments are administered and the evaluator wishes to minimize redundancy, but is perhaps better retained even when both are administered as a sort of internal consistency check: Does the respondent offer similar priorities in two separate instances?

Like other instruments provided here, "**Parenting Capacity Semi-Structured Interview / Parenting Capacity Questionnaire**" is not scored. Although the evaluator may see some items as obviously true or false (e.g., Item #10: "It's normal for children to test limits"), answers are not graded in any fashion. In this instances, the fact that every other item is highlighted only intends to facilitate reading and responding. Answers are only used qualitatively to characterize the respondent's parenting beliefs and professed practices and for comparison to the respondent's co-parent's positions in the same matters.

With regard to the latter: It is reasonable to infer that co-parents with dramatically different parenting beliefs and practices are likely to have significant co-parenting conflict. Even if they are able to communicate and cooperate, the consistency of their parenting practices will be very poor. A child migrating between such parents may experience a kind of culture shock adjusting from one environment to another and then back again frequently. It is, however, not reasonable to infer that parents who espouse similar parenting practices and beliefs are necessarily good co-parents.

Semi-structured Parenting Capacity Interview
Page 1 of 11

Parenting Capacity Semi-Structured Interview

© 2015 Benjamin D. Garber, Ph.D.

To the evaluator: This instrument prompts questions related to an adult's parenting beliefs, attitudes and practices. These questions are intentionally generic, that is, they are not about any particular child.

In part A, the respondent is asked about each of eight factors known to be parenting risks. In any instance in which a risk is acknowledged, it is important to explore further. Insight into the risk can mitigate the risk: Does the adult recognize that the matter being discussed bears on parenting? Action to correct the risk further mitigates the risk: What is the respondent doing to optimize his or her parenting capacity?

In Part B, the respondent is asked offer a response from "strongly agree" to "strongly disagree" to each of eight parenting belief statements. Responses correspond to Baumrind's (1991) parenting types.

This interview format is intended to serve as one part of a larger parenting competence and capacity evaluation. The respondent's answers to the prompts provided here should be followed up in interview and, when possible and appropriate, by seeking objective records and corroborating third-party reports. In some instances, responses can later be contrasted with observations of the adult's actual behavior with his or her child.

"Insight" means a spontaneous recognition of the potential impact of the factor on present-day parenting attitudes, beliefs or practices.

"...an awareness of one's role as a parent, including understanding your individual child, their needs, and your ability to provide for those needs... [and a willingness to] acknowledge limitations as a parent"

(Eve et al., 2014)

Semi-structured Parenting Capacity Interview
Page 2 of 11

A. Parenting Risks and Supports

Caregiving attitude, belief or practice	✓ if this domain is a concern	Does the respondent have insight into this domain?	Is the respondent actively working on this domain?
1. Personal Trauma History			
Does the respondent have a history of trauma of any kind? This includes abuse, neglect and traumatic loss? How, if at all, does the respondent see these experiences as relevant to parenting in the present?			

A history of trauma can put a parent at risk for recreating similar abuse and neglect.

Insight into this possibility, education and healthy community support mitigate against this outcome.

"…some mothers and fathers with a history of child abuse may benefit from parenting interventions that address difficulties with emotional disengagement.

Specific attention could be paid to assist these parents with emotional regulation strategies to maximize their emotional and physical engagement with their child, so as to increase their capacity for availability, time spent with the child, and parental self-efficacy."
(Ehrensaft et al., 2015)

"….unresolved childhood trauma in the parent poses a known risk for later maltreatment of children in adulthood…."

(Farnfield, 2008;

See also Banyard, 1997; DiLillo & Damashek, 2003)

Semi-Structured Parenting Capacity Interview
Page 3 of 11

Caregiving attitude, belief or practice	✓ If this domain is a concern	Does the respondent have insight into this domain?	Is the respondent actively working on this domain?
2. **Health Concerns & Limits**			
Does the respondent have any current physical health or mental health concerns? How, if at all, does the respondent see these as relevant to parenting in the present?			

Chronic physical and/or mental illness and/or current or past substance addiction can negatively impact parenting.

Insight into this problem, proper physical and mental health care and community support mitigate against this prospect.

"...ex-drinkers to frequent heavy drinkers used physically abusive parenting practices more often than lifetime abstainers."

(Freisthler et al., 2014)

Semi-Structured Parenting Capacity Interview
Page 4 of 11

Caregiving attitude, belief or practice	✓ domain is a concern	Does the respondent have insight into this domain?	Is the respondent actively working on this domain?
3. **Positive Role Model** Does the respondent see him- or herself as a positive role model to a child? In what ways? a. Smoking, alcohol and substance use? b. Profanity, bullying and prejudice? c. Impulsivity and violence? d. Diet and exercise? e. Reading and education? f. Responsibility, reliability and follow-through?			

Children do as their parents do far more often than they do what their parents say.

A parent who is impulsive and has trouble delaying gratification is at high risk for abuse, neglect and modeling inappropriate behaviors.

"…[results suggest that] treatment for parental ADHD may impact parenting performance, and suggest that attention to parental ADHD in treatment for adolescents with ADHD may possibly enhance family functioning"

(Babinski et al., 2014)

"The effect of maternal remission on the child's improvement was partially explained by an improvement in the mother's parenting, particularly the change in the mother's ability to listen and talk to her child, but also reflected in her improvement in parental bonding."

(Weissman et al., 2014)

(Regarding chronic illness and parenting see Ackerson, 2003; Regarding impulsivity and substance abuse see Matusiewicz, et al., 2013)

Semi-Structured Parenting Capacity Interview
Page 5 of 11

Caregiving attitude, belief or practice	✓ if this domain is a concern	Does the respondent have insight into this domain?	Is the respondent actively working on this domain?
4. Cognitive skills			
Does the respondent see him- or herself as able to understand, organize and advocate for a child? Are language skills impaired?			

Cognitive limitations can negatively impact parenting capacity, particularly in areas of executive function and self-regulation (e.g., Llewellyn et al., 2003; Booth et al., 2005; McGaw et al., 2010).

For a provocative if non-scientific perspective, see "I Am Sam" (2001, New Line Cinema).

Does the respondent have a learning disability (LD)?

LD usually means that the individual has measurably greater intellectual abilities in one area of functioning than in another.

Inquire about these differences: Does the respondent have greater difficulty with verbal or non-verbal tasks? Spoken or written language? Math or reading or writing?

LD is quite distinct from cognitive delay or "mental retardation."
(Learn more: MacLean & Aunos, 2010; Feldman et al., 2012; Feldman & Aunos, 2011; Bloomfield et al., 2010)

Semi-Structured Parenting Capacity Interview
Page 6 of 11

Caregiving attitude, belief or practice	✓ If this domain is a concern	Does the respondent have insight into this domain?	Is the respondent actively working on this domain?
5. **Material resources**			
Does the respondent believe that he or she has the financial and material resources necessary to care for a child?			

Poverty negatively impacts parenting in part as a result of associated depression, anxiety, anger and substance abuse (e.g., Henninger et al., 2014).

The negative impact of poverty on parenting can be compounded by neighborhood stressors (e.g., Barajas-Gonzalez et al., 2014).

Ask further:

- **What is the effect of perceived poverty on respondent's mood and behavior?**
- **What is the effect of perceived poverty on housing, vehicle and safety?**
- **What is the effect of perceived poverty on access to healthcare and education?**
- **What is the effect of perceived poverty on neighborhood safety?**

Semi-structured Parenting Capacity Interview
Page 7 of 11

Semi-Structured Parenting Capacity Interview
Page 7 of 11

Caregiving attitude, belief or practice	✓ if this domain is a concern	Does the respondent have insight into this domain?	Is the respondent actively working on this domain?
6. Healthy adult social supports			
Does the respondent have a network of positive and appropriate friends, relatives and/or professionals for emotional support, advice and practical assistance?			

Parents' "social capital" can mitigate other stresses to the child's and family's benefit (e.g., Richardson et al., 2014).

What about parents' use of social networking sites? (e.g., Doty & Dworkin, 2014).

Intellectual disabilities can exacerbate isolation and family stress (e.g., Darbyshire & Stenfert Kroese, 2012).

For young parents, in particular:

"… social support and family functioning during pregnancy were associated with a greater sense of parenting competence, and these associations were mediated by parental depression."

(Angley et al., 2014)

"Parents who receive support from family, friends, community or faith-based activities are both physically and psychologically stronger than those who do not … and are likely to offer a more positive caregiving environment."
(Farnfield, 2008)

75

Semi-Structured Parenting Capacity Interview
Page 8 of 11

	✓ domain is a concern	Does the respondent have insight into this domain?	Is the respondent actively working on this domain?
Caregiving attitude, belief or practice			
7. Community affiliation			
Is the respondent affiliated with any community group, organization or affiliation? Examples include church, synagogue or masque; schools, libraries, support groups			

Parents' active participation in their children's schools can mitigate family stress and facilitate achievement (e.g., Sime & Sheridan, 2014).

"Although survival after childhood is possible without a complex network of social relationships, both physical and psychological functioning are seriously compromised in those who are socially isolated." (Gleason & Narvaez, 2014)

Neighborhood supports create critical social capital and can help to mitigate parenting and family stress (e.g., Carpiano & Kimbro, 2012).

Ask about neighborhoods:

- **Do you live in a neighborhood?**
- **Do you know your neighbors by name?**
- **Do you socialize with people in your neighborhood?**
- **Would you feel comfortable asking a neighbor to help out in an emergency?**

Semi-Structured Parenting Capacity Interview
Page 9 of 11

Caregiving attitude, belief or practice	✓ If this is a concern	Does the respondent have insight into this domain?	respondent actively working on this domain?
8. Cultural affiliations			
Does the respondent identify with a cultural, religious or language group?			

When parents belong to and feel supported by others of similar cultural, religious and/or language groups, family stresses can be mitigated.

Conversely, parents who feel culturally isolated may be more stressed with a negative impact on parenting and child well-being.

Pantin et al., (2007) discuss…"…protective factors may offset the effects of risks associated with immigration, disadvantage, cultural isolation, and parent-adolescent acculturation differences, and they may help to prevent adolescent substance abuse and delinquency."

A parent who feels isolated and apart from the surrounding community is at high stress. His or her child is at higher risk for both abuse and adultification.

Ask about cultural affiliations:

- **Do you have friends who share your cultural identity? Your language or religion?**
- **Who do you spend time with that is similar to you?**
- **Who do you celebrate holidays with?**
- **What language is spoken in your home? What religion is practiced?**

Semi-structured Parenting Capacity Interview
Page 10-11 of 11

B. Parenting attitudes and beliefs

Ask the respondent to respond on a 0-4 scale from strongly agree to strongly disagree for each of the following statements	Strongly agree 4	3	Not sure 2	1	Strongly disagree 0
9 Emotional attunement "I believe that a parent should be very tuned into a child's emotions, even when the child says nothing."					
10 Reliable "I believe that a child should be able to count on his or her parent to be present and responsive when needed."					
11 Empathic "I believe that a parent should be able to identify and support a child's emotional experiences, even when that child is angry, sad or scared."					
12 Directive "I believe that a parent should make his or her expectations clear and firm to the child."					

Ask the respondent to respond on a 0-4 scale from strongly agree to strongly disagree for each of the following statements	Strongly agree 4	3	Not sure 2	1	Strongly disagree 0
13 Assertive "I believe that a parent should pick his or her battles."					
14 Follow through "I believe that if a parent sets a limit, it is important to follow through with any associated reward or punishment."					
15 Control "I believe that a parent should be willing to explain his or her reasoning to a child."					
16 Respect "I believe that child's words, interests, feelings and possessions should be respected as his or her own."					

Interpreting these responses in terms of Baumrind's (2013) four parenting types

(numbers in parentheses refer to items on the two pages captured above):

Permissive parenting

High attunement (9)

Low reliability (10)

Low empathic (11)

Low directive (12)

Low assertive (13)

Low follow through (14)

Low control (15)

High respect (16)

Authoritative parenting

High attunement (9)

Highly reliable (10)

Highly empathic (11)

Highly directive (12)

Highly assertive (13)

High follow through (14)

Confrontative control (15)

High respect (16)

Control

———————————————————— Support ————————————————————

Low attunement (9)

Low reliability (10)

Low empathy (11)

Low directive (12)

Low assertive (13)

Low follow through (14)

Low control (15)

Low respect (16)

Disengaged parenting

Low attunement (9)

Highly reliable (10)

Low empathy (11)

Highly directive (12)

Highly assertive (13)

High follow through (14)

Coercive control (15)

Low respect (16)

Authoritarian parenting

FORM 7: Parenting Capacity Semi-Structured Interview / Parenting Capacity Questionnaire
Page 1 of 5

Parenting Capacity Questionnaire
© 2013 Benjamin D. Garber, Ph.D.

About You (please check ALL that are true):

I am:
- ☐ Birth parent
- ☐ Step-parent
- ☐ Foster/adoptive parent
- ☐ Legal guardian
- ☐ Unrelated, live-in co-parent

- ☐ less than 25 years old
- ☐ 26-40 years old
- ☐ 41 or older

- ☐ Male
- ☐ Female

I currently share at least some of my parenting responsibilities with another adult: ☐ TRUE ☐ FALSE

The oldest child that I parent is: _____ years old

The youngest child that I parent is: _____ years old

Please respond to each item below by indicating your agreement in general. These items are NOT about you or your children specifically. They are about your parenting beliefs in general.

Please respond to each item indicating whether you believe that the statement is TRUE or FALSE.

Feel free to add comments on the reverse of each page.

For example:

99. Children are younger than their parents. ☑ TRUE ☐ FALSE

1. Parents must teach their children what is right and what is wrong. ☐ TRUE ☐ FALSE

2. Children need to feel loved no matter what. ☐ TRUE ☐ FALSE

This is a forced choice instrument.

Respondents are asked to respond either true or false.

Many will nonetheless add comments, conditions and/or mark between true and false.

Because the instrument is not scored or normed, this is all data to be explored.

But aren't there objective TRUE and FALSE realities about child development and parenting?

Yes. Unless you are using this instrument as a final exam in a college course, objective reality doesn't matter as much as understanding the respondent's parenting attitudes, beliefs and behaviors and (when appropriate) comparing these to a co-parent's responses within the limits of safety. Responses that suggest attitudes, beliefs or practices likely to endanger a child must be thoroughly explored in follow-up interview.

FORM 7: Parenting Capacity Semi-Structured Interview / Parenting Capacity Questionnaire

Page 2 of 5

Parenting Capacity Questionnaire

3.	It's okay for parents to keep secrets with their children from the other parent.	☐ TRUE ☐ FALSE
4.	Children feel good about themselves if their parents express pride in them.	☐ TRUE ☐ FALSE
5.	Limits on children's behavior inhibit their creativity.	☐ TRUE ☐ FALSE
6.	When children say, "I don't care" parents must understand that the child genuinely does not care.	☐ TRUE ☐ FALSE
7.	Children need a predictable schedule.	☐ TRUE ☐ FALSE
8.	When a child says, "I hate you!" parents must understand that the child probably means, "I'm mad at you!"	☐ TRUE ☐ FALSE
9.	Play is one way in which children cope with stress	☐ TRUE ☐ FALSE
10.	It is normal for children to test limits	☐ TRUE ☐ FALSE
11.	Parents must communicate actively with children's teachers and doctors.	☐ TRUE ☐ FALSE
12.	Punishments should be predictable.	☐ TRUE ☐ FALSE
13.	Parents must never intrude on children's privacy.	☐ TRUE ☐ FALSE
14.	Stress can cause a child to behave in a less mature way.	☐ TRUE ☐ FALSE
15.	Children must never be exposed to adult conflict	☐ TRUE ☐ FALSE
16.	Parents must help their children express strong feelings.	☐ TRUE ☐ FALSE
17.	Children often copy their parents' behavior.	☐ TRUE ☐ FALSE
18.	Children must earn their parents' love.	☐ TRUE ☐ FALSE

Page 2 of 5

Comments by item number:

7. TRUE may bear on how rigid or flexible a parenting plan needs to be

8. FALSE raises questions about the parent's maturity and stress.

11. Bears on parent's advocacy or subjective helplessness

13. How are boundaries defined in this family? Test further: What about an emergency? What if you thought she was using drugs?

14. FALSE: How does this parent understand and respond to neediness?

17. Does the parent recognize him- or herself as a model that child emulates?

18. If TRUE, how is love earned or lost?

FORM 7: Parenting Capacity Semi-Structured Interview / Parenting Capacity Questionnaire
Page 3 of 5

Parenting Capacity Questionnaire

#	Item	True	False
19.	Spanking can be an effective means of teaching children what is right from what is wrong	☐ TRUE	☐ FALSE
20.	"Time out" can be an effective means of teaching children what is right from what is wrong	☐ TRUE	☐ FALSE
21.	"Grounding" can be an effective means of teaching children what is right from what is wrong	☐ TRUE	☐ FALSE
22.	Punishing works better than rewarding as a means of teaching children what is right from what is wrong.	☐ TRUE	☐ FALSE
23.	Parents must try to answer all of their children's questions completely and honestly.	☐ TRUE	☐ FALSE
24.	Children need the opportunity to have a healthy relationship with both of their parents.	☐ TRUE	☐ FALSE
25.	Children need rules.	☐ TRUE	☐ FALSE
26.	At some ages, children normally become more defiant and rebellious.	☐ TRUE	☐ FALSE
27.	Children's needs change as they grow.	☐ TRUE	☐ FALSE
28.	At some ages, children need their fathers more than their mothers.	☐ TRUE	☐ FALSE
29.	Parents must carefully monitor children's media (TV, internet, radio, music).	☐ TRUE	☐ FALSE
30.	Children don't experience anger, sadness or fear until they are 5 years old or older.	☐ TRUE	☐ FALSE
31.	Children can't remember experiences before 5 years old	☐ TRUE	☐ FALSE
32.	Teenagers need mothers more than fathers.	☐ TRUE	☐ FALSE
33.	Children have no interest in sexual exploration before adolescence.	☐ TRUE	☐ FALSE
34.	Children must be taught not to be angry.	☐ TRUE	☐ FALSE

Page 3 of 5

Spanking?

"…the lasting effects of early spanking, both in influencing early child's behavior, and in affecting subsequent child's externalizing and parental spanking in a reciprocal manner"

(Mackenzie et al., 2014).

Comments by item number:

19-22 (and see 12, 37, 41) all ask about punishment. Does the respondent believe in spanking? (See sidebar below)

24. FALSE raises questions about estrangement and alienation.

28, 32 (and 35) ask about parent-child gender matching. Generally it is true that every child has periods when he or she needs a same and an opposite gender role-model, as well as a model of healthy adult relationships.

27, 30, 33 and 42 ask about the respondent's awareness of development and individual differences among children…

34 (and see 16) ask whether strong feelings are allowed or forbidden.

Parenting Capacity Questionnaire

		TRUE / FALSE
35.	Boys need fathers more than girls need fathers.	☐ TRUE ☐ FALSE
36.	Children feel more secure when their parents cooperate with each other.	☐ TRUE ☐ FALSE
37.	A child who hits should be hit back.	☐ TRUE ☐ FALSE
38.	Children need to know the complete truth about their parents' relationship.	☐ TRUE ☐ FALSE
39.	A parent who establishes a rule must follow through with the rule.	☐ TRUE ☐ FALSE
40.	Children should be allowed to make their own decisions.	☐ TRUE ☐ FALSE
41.	Ignoring a child ("the silent treatment") is an effective punishment.	☐ TRUE ☐ FALSE
42.	Every physically healthy child is the same at birth.	☐ TRUE ☐ FALSE
43.	Parents should make their children's happiness their first priority.	☐ TRUE ☐ FALSE
44.	There are times when parents must force their children to do things that the children don't want to do.	☐ TRUE ☐ FALSE
45.	A parent must never "give in" to a child's whining, pleading and begging.	☐ TRUE ☐ FALSE
46.	Children should be seen but not heard.	☐ TRUE ☐ FALSE
47.	Parents should follow their children's lead in play.	☐ TRUE ☐ FALSE
48.	Mothers are always better caregivers than fathers.	☐ TRUE ☐ FALSE
49.	Parents should always fully and accurately answer when children ask "why?"	☐ TRUE ☐ FALSE
50.	Parents must always follow through with limits and consequences even when children whine and tantrum.	☐ TRUE ☐ FALSE

Page 4 of 5

Comments by item number:

38. TRUE raises questions about boundaries and the risk of adultification.

36. TRUE suggests child-centered priorities and a willingness to cooperate with other caregiver (see also 24 TRUE)

40. TRUE (and 25 FALSE and 44 FALSE) suggests a permissive or disengaged parenting style.

50 and 39 TRUE suggests authoritative or authoritarian parenting.

Parenting Capacity Questionnaire

51. Please rank the following statements from 1 to 10 to indicate your parenting priorities.
Rank the most important item = 1.
Rank the second most important item = 2, and so on.
Rank the least important item = 10.
Please use each number only once.

The item that you feel is most important	= 1
The item that you feel is second most important	= 2
	.
	.
The item that you feel is least important	= 10

Item	Your priority
The child's happiness	
The parent's happiness	
The child's health	
The parent's health	
The child's wishes and wants	
The adult's wishes and wants	
The safety of the home	
The comfort of the home	
How much the parent earns	
How much the child likes the parent	

Please feel free to add any comments on the back of any page.

Thank you

Page 5 of 5

Consider:

Which is a higher priority to the parent:

1. Health or happiness?
2. Parent or child well-being?
3. How do comfort and wealth weigh in?

How much does the parent need to feel "liked" by the child?

When this is an acknowledged priority, it's important to question how the parent tolerates the child's anger and how this bears on limits and consequences.

(See also the more elaborate parenting priorities worksheet in the

"Individual Caregiver Personal and Parenting History" (page 27)

References

Abidin, R. R., Flens, J. T., & Austin, W. G. (2006). The parenting stress index. In R. Archer (Ed.), *Forensic uses of clinical assessment instruments* (pp. 297–328). Mahwah, NJ: Erlbaum.

Ackerson, B. J. (2003) Coping with the dual demands of severe mental illness and parenting: the parents' perspective. *Family in Society*, 84, 109-118.

Ainsworth, M. (2010). Security and attachment. In R. Volpe (Ed.), *The secure child: Timeless lessons in parenting and childhood education* (pp. 43-53). Charlotte, NC: Information Age Publishing.

Alt, Dorit (2014). First-year female college students' academic motivation as a function of perceived parenting styles: A contextual perspective. *Journal of Adult Development.*

Angley, Meghan; Divney, Anna; Magriples, Urania & Kershaw, Trace (2014). Social support, family functioning and parenting competence in adolescent parents. *Maternal and Child Health Journal*, 19(1):67-73.

Babinski, Dara E.; Waxmonsky, James G.; Waschbusch, Daniel A.; Humphrey, Hugh; Alfonso, Alexandra; Crum, Kathleen I.; Bernstein, Melissa; Slavec, Janine; Augustus, Juhea N &; Pelham Jr., William E. (2014). A pilot study of stimulant medication for adults with attention-deficit/hyperactivity disorder (ADHD) who are parents of adolescents with ADHD: The acute effects of stimulant medication on observed parent-adolescent interactions. *Journal of Child and Adolescent Psychopharmacology*, 24(10), 582-585.

Banyard, V. L. (1997). The impact of childhood sexual abuse and family functioning on four dimensions of women's later parenting. *Child Abuse and Neglect*, 21(11), 1095-1107.

Barajas-Gonzalez, R. Gabriela & Brooks-Gunn, Jeanne (2014). Income, neighborhood stressors, and harsh parenting: Test of moderation by ethnicity, age, and gender. *Journal of Family Psychology*, 28(6), 855-866.

Baumrind, D. H. (1991). The influence of parenting style on adolescent competence and substance use. *Journal of Early Adolescence*, 11, 56-95.

Baumrind, Diana (2013). Is a pejorative view of power assertion in the socialization process justified? *Review of General Psychology*, 17(4), 420-427.

Becoña, Elisardo; Martínez, Úrsula; Calafat, Amador; Fernández-Hermida, Ramón José; Juan, Montse; Sumnall, Harry; Mendes, Fernando; Gabrhelík, Roman

(2013). Parental permissiveness, control, and affect and drug use among adolescents. *Psicothema*, 25(3), 292-298.

Beijersbergen, M. D. Juffer, F. Bakermans-Kranenburg, M. J. van IJzendoorn, M. H. (2012). Remaining or becoming secure: Parental sensitive support predicts attachment continuity from infancy to adolescence in a longitudinal adoption study. *Developmental Psychology*, 48, 1277-1282.

Bloomfield, Linda; Kendall, Sally & Fortuna, Sandra (2010). Supporting parents: Development of a tool to measure self-efficacy of parents with learning disabilities. *British Journal of Learning Disabilities*, 38(4), 303-309

Booth, T. Booth, W. McConnell, D. (2005). The prevalence and outcomes of care proceedings involving parents with learning difficulties in the family courts. *Journal of Applied Research in Intellectual Disabilities*, 18, 7-17.

Carpiano, R. M. & Kimbro, R. T. (2012). Neighborhood social capital, parenting strain, and personal mastery among female primary caregivers of children. *J Health Soc Behav.* 2012; 53(2):232-247.

Choate, Peter W. & Engstrom, Sandra (2014). The "Good Enough" Parent: Implications for Child Protection. *Child Care in Practice*, 20(4), 368-382.

Darbyshire, L. V. Stenfert Kroese, B. (2012). Psychological well-being and social support for parents with intellectual disabilities: Risk factors and interventions. *Journal of Police and Practice in Intellectual Disabilities*, 9(1), 40-52.

DiLillo, D. & Damashek, A. (2003). Parenting characteristics of women reporting a history of childhood sexual abuse. *Child Maltreatment*, 8(4), 319-333.

Doty, Jennifer & Dworkin, Jodi (2014). Parents' of adolescents' use of social networking sites. *Computers in Human Behavior*, 33, 349-355.

Ehrensaft, Miriam K.; Knous-Westfall, Heather M.; Cohen, Patricia; Chen, Henian (2015). How does child abuse history influence parenting of the next generation? *Psychology of Violence*, 5(1), 16-25.

Eve, Philippa M.; Byrne, Mitchell K.; Gagliardi, Cinzia R. (2014). What is good parenting? The perspectives of different professionals. *Family Court Review*, 52(1), 114-127.

Farnfield, Steve (2008). A theoretical model for the comprehensive assessment of parenting. *British Journal of Social Work*, 38(6), 1076-1099.

Fearon, Danielle D.; Copeland, Daelynn; Saxon, Terrill F. (2013). The relationship between parenting styles and creativity in a sample of Jamaican children. *Creativity Research Journal*, 25(1), 119-128.

Feldman, M. McConnell, D. Aunos, M. (2012). Parental cognitive impairment, mental health and child outcomes in a child protection population. *Journal of Mental Health Research in Intellectual Disabilities* 2012; 5:66-90.

Feldman, Maurice &; Aunos, Marjorie (2011). *Comprehensive, competence-based parenting assessment for parents with learning difficulties and their children.* Kingston, NY, US: NADD Press.

Freisthler, Bridget; Holmes, Megan R.; Wolf, Jennifer Price (2014). The dark side of social support: Understanding the role of social support, drinking behaviors and alcohol outlets for child physical abuse. *Child Abuse & Neglect*, 38(6), 1106-1119.

Georgiou, Stelios N.; Fousiani, Kyriaki; Michaelides, Michalis; Stavrinides, Panayiotis (2013). Cultural value orientation and authoritarian parenting as parameters of bullying and victimization at school. *International Journal of Psychology*, 48(1), 69-78.

Gleason, Tracy R. & Narvaez, Darcia (2014). Childhood environments and flourishing. In Narvaez, Darcia; Valentino, Kristin; Fuentes, Agustin; McKenna, James J. & Gray, Peter (Eds.), (2014). *Ancestral landscapes in human evolution: Culture, childrearing and social wellbeing.* , (pp. 335-348). New York, NY, US: Oxford University Press.

Henninger IV, William R.; Luze, Gayle (2014). Poverty, caregiver depression and stress as predictors of children's externalizing behaviours in a low-income sample. *Child & Family Social Work*, 19(4), 467-479.

Hibbard, D.R.; Walton, G.E. (2014). Exploring the development of perfectionism: The influence of parenting style and gender. *Social Behavior and Personality*, 42(2), 269-278.

Hoffmann, John P.; Bahr, Stephen J. (2014). Parenting style, religiosity, peer alcohol use, and adolescent heavy drinking. *Journal of Studies on Alcohol and Drugs*, 75(2), 222-227.

Huang, Ching-Yu; Lamb, Michael E. (2015). Acculturation and parenting in first-generation Chinese immigrants in the United Kingdom. *Journal of Cross-Cultural Psychology*, 46(1), 150-167.

Hurley, K.D.; Huscroft-D'Angelo, J.; Trout, A.; Griffith, A.; Epstein, M. (2014). Assessing parenting skills and attitudes: A review of the psychometrics of parenting measures. *Journal of Child and Family Studies*, 23(5), 812-823.

LeCuyer-Maus, E. A. (2000). Maternal sensitivity and responsiveness, limit-setting style, and relationship history in the transition to toddlerhood. *Issues in Comprehensive Pediatric Nursing,* 23, 117-139.

Llewellyn, G. McConnell, D. Ferronato, L. (2003). Prevalence and outcomes for parents with disabilities and their children in an Australian court sample. *Child Abuse & Neglect,* 27, 235-251.

MacKenzie, Michael J.; Nicklas, Eric; Brooks-Gunn, Jeanne& Waldfogel, Jane (2014). Repeated exposure to high-frequency spanking and child externalizing behavior across the first decade: A moderating role for cumulative risk. *Child Abuse & Neglect,* 38(12), 1895-1901.

MacLean, Katie & Aunos, Marjorie (2010). Addressing the needs of parents with intellectual disabilities: Exploring a parenting pilot project. *Journal on Developmental Disabilities,* 16(1), 18-33

Matusiewicz, Alexis K.; Macatee, Richard J.; Guller, Leila; Lejuez, C. W. (2013). Impulsivity and addiction in parents. In Suchman, Nancy E.; Pajulo, Marjukka & Mayes, Linda C. (Eds.), Parenting and substance abuse: *Developmental approaches to intervention.* New York, NY, US: Oxford University Press.

McGaw, S.; Scully, T. & Pritchard, C. (2010). Predicting the unpredictable? Identifying high-risk versus low-risk parents with intellectual disabilities. *Child Abuse & Neglect,* 34, 699-710.

Miller, A. L. Lambert, A. D. Speirs Neumeister, K. L. (2012). Parenting style, perfectionism, and creativity in high-ability and high-achieving young adults. *Journal for the Education of the Gifted,* 35, 344-365.

Moses Passini, Christina; Pihet, Sandrine & Favez, Nicolas (2014). Assessing specific discipline techniques: A mixed-methods approach. *Journal of Child and Family Studies,* 23(8), 1389-1402.

Nelson, David A.; Coyne, Sarah M.; Swanson, Savannah M.; Hart, Craig H.; Olsen, Joseph A. (2014). Parenting, relational aggression, and borderline personality features: Associations over time in a Russian longitudinal sample. *Development and Psychopathology,* 26(3), 773-787.

Pantin, H. Schwartz, S. J. Coatsworth, J. D. (2007). Familias unidas: A systemic, parent-centered approach to preventing problem behavior in Hispanic adolescents. In: Szapocznik J Tolan P Sambrano S (Eds). *Preventing Youth Substance Abuse: Science-Based Programs for Children and Adolescents.* Washington, DC: American Psychological Association; 2007: 211-238.

Pezzot-Pearce, T. & Pearce, J. (2004). *Parenting Assessments in Child Welfare Cases: A Practical Guide.* Toronto, Canada: University of Toronto Press

Richardson Jr., Joseph B.; Johnson Jr., Waldo E. & St. Vil, Christopher (2014). I want him locked up: Social capital, African American parenting strategies, and the juvenile court. *Journal of Contemporary Ethnography*, 43(4), 488-522.

Sime, Daniela & Sheridan, Marion (2014). 'You want the best for your kids': Improving educational outcomes for children living in poverty through parental engagement. *Educational Research*, 56(3), 327-342.

Trifan, Tatiana Alina; Stattin, Håkan; Tilton-Weaver, Lauree (2014). Have authoritarian parenting practices and roles changed in the last 50 years? *Journal of Marriage and Family*, 76(4), 744-761.

Uji, Masayo; Sakamoto, Ayuko; Adachi, Keiichiro; Kitamura, Toshinori (2014). The impact of authoritative, authoritarian, and permissive parenting styles on children's later mental health in Japan: Focusing on parent and child gender. *Journal of Child and Family Studies*, 23(2), 293-302.

Varvil-Weld, Lindsey; Crowley, D. Max; Turrisi, Rob; Greenberg, Mark T.; Mallett, Kimberly A. (2014). Hurting, helping, or neutral? The effects of parental permissiveness toward adolescent drinking on college student alcohol use and problems. *Prevention Science*, 15(5), 716-724.

Watabe, Akiko; Hibbard, David R. (2014). The influence of authoritarian and authoritative parenting on children's academic achievement motivation: A comparison between the United States and Japan. *North American Journal of Psychology*, 16(2), 359-382.

Weissman, M. M.; Wickramaratne, P.; Pilowsky, D. J.; Poh, E.; Hernandez, M.; Batten, L. A.; Flament, M. F.; Stewart, J. W.; Blier, P. (2014). The effects on children of depressed mothers' remission and relapse over 9 months. *Psychological Medicine*, 44(13), 2811-2824.

F. Caregiver's View of the Child

Rationale and uses

No matter the evaluator's experience, expertise or investment in any particular evaluation, the obvious fact is that the parents will always know more about the child. However, eliciting a parent's wealth of information can be as challenging as it is important. No parent can ever be entirely without bias when speaking of his or her child. Thus, the evaluator is once again required to separate the wheat from the chaff; the facts from the biases.

Two questionnaires are presented here. Each serves the purpose of eliciting the caregiver's view of his or her child. Both lend themselves to two types of scrutiny in search of the "chaff:" When administered to two of more caregivers who share responsibility to a single child, the adult responses can be compared item-by-item. Similarities highlight points of co-parental convergence and suggest (but by no means assure) that a particular observation may be accurate. Differences can reflect different experiences with the child, different expectations and biases (lenses) through which the child is seen, and can reflect genuine differences in the child's chameleon-like presentation to the respondents (Garber,2014).

Caregiver responses on each of these two instruments can be compared to the child's own responses, presentation and/or to the reports of third parties (e.g., teachers, neighbors, therapists, physicians). Similarities here again suggest (but still don't assure) accuracy. Differences must be sorted through one item at a time, weighing the child's motivations in direct interview, third parties' limited experiences and caregiver biases.

"The Child's World Questionnaire" assesses a respondent's familiarity with the child's evident and admitted preferences and favorites. There is nothing scientific or empirically derived here. The premise is simply that children feel good about themselves when their caregivers express an interest in their world. A parent who can accurately identify the child's favorite ice cream flavor and best friend, for example, may be demonstrating impressive sensitivity on one hand, or perhaps a child-like enmeshment on the other.

A parent who knows none of the details of the child's world and perhaps even dismisses the questions as unimportant, may be disengaged. The evaluator reasonably wonders how the child feels in that adult's care, whether perhaps he or she feels compelled (or invited) to engage the adult in adult matters, i.e., becomes adultified or parentified.

The accompanying "**Child Cross Check Interview**" can be used as an interview tool with the child or, in some instances, can be assigned as homework between interviews. The questions match the adult's questions. Beware parental interference any time a child is asked to complete a questionnaire outside the evaluator's direct observation.

The **"Perceptions of My Child (and Summary Sheet)"** questionnaire asks the caregiver to indicate how much each of forty-six statements are true of the child. Responses requested on a 1-10 scale where 1=never and 10=always. A record scoring and interpretation page follows with which the evaluator can actively compare and contrast parents' responses.

FORM 8: The Child's World Questionnaire
Page 1-2 of 2

The Child's World
© 2015 Benjamin D. Garber, Ph.D.

Successful parenting routinely requires an adult to develop a sense of how the child sees the world: What and who the child likes and dislikes, his or her preferences, favorites, skills, wishes and fears.

A separate questionnaire must be completed regarding each child individually.

My name: _____   Today's Date: _____

I am completing this questionnaire regarding
(child's full name): _____

My present role in this child's life is :
(Father? Step-mother? Grandmother? Foster-parent?) _____

This child is in my care _____ percentage of the
time: _____ % of time in my care

1. This child is:

_____ right handed

_____ left handed

_____ no clear preference
(too young or ambidextrous)

Please identify this child's "favorite" for each category named at left. For example:
Category
Example: Vegetable   His or her favorite is...

_____ *broccoli* _____

2. Song: _____

3. Television show: _____

4. Movie: _____

5. Color: _____

6. Sport: _____

The Child's World   page 2

Category   His or her favorite is...
7. Ice cream flavor: _____

8. Book: _____

9. Toy: _____

10. How does this child comfort him-
or herself when distressed? _____

11. What would this child say scares
him or her? _____
12. Who is this child's hero? _____

13. How would this child answer,
"What do you want to be when
you grow up?" _____
14. Who is this child's best friend? _____

15. What is this child's favorite part
of school? _____
16. Who else would this child name
among his or her close friends? _____

_____

_____

17. What makes this child MAD
when in your care? _____
18. What makes this child SAD when
in your care? _____
19. What makes this child HAPPY
when in your care? _____
20. What makes this child SCARED
when in your care? _____

Consider:

1. Some questions seek information that should be stable and certain (e.g., #1 about handedness)

2. Children's interests and preferences emerge and disappear rapidly. A parent who is recently out of touch with a child (e.g., in the case of contact resistance) may not be up to date. In fact, some children's preferences will shift during the course of a single school day.

3. Questions 10 and 17-20 ask about the child's emotional experiences. Credible and accurate responses may suggest adult sensitivity.

4. Question 12 seems to tap something essential and needed among parents who are separating, divorcing and otherwise anxious. Many respond "me." In some cases, they may even be correct.

5. Question 16 can be very telling. Does the caregiver know the child's friends? Beware that when children split their time between homes, they sometimes have two sets of friends. If child and parent answers diverge, ask the child about "the other house."

FORM 9: The Child's World Questionnaire: Child Cross-Check Interview

Page 1-2 of 2

Page 1

The Child's World:
Child Cross-Check Interview
© 2015 Benjamin D. Garber, Ph.D.

Evaluator: Eliciting responses to the following questions can help to validate adult responses. These questions can be asked in face-to-face interview or assigned as homework for the child. Beware that the child's responses are his or her won, untainted by a proximal parent, sibling or environment.

Child's Name: _____

Child's Date of Birth: _____ Age: _____

Today's Date: _____ Evaluator admin? Y N

Child Accompanied by: _____ HW Admin Y N

1. I am:
  _____ right handed
  _____ left handed
  _____ no clear preference

Please identify your favorite...

2. Song:
3. Television show:
4. Movie:
5. Color:
6. Sport:
7. Ice cream flavor:
8. Book:
9. Toy:

Page 2

The Child's World   page 2

10. What do you do to feel better when you're upset?

11. What scares you?

12. Who is your hero?

13. "What do you want to be when you grow up?

14. Who is your BFF or best friend?

15. What is your favorite part of school?

16. What are the first names of your other close friends?

	When you're with DAD?	When you're with MOM?
17. What makes you MAD		
18. What makes you SAD?		
19. What makes you HAPPY		
20. What makes you SCARED?		

The proximal environment can be very influential.

The evaluator must take into account who transported the child to interview, how long they may have sat together in the car in transit, whether the child fears that a parent waiting in an adjoining room can overhear the interview, what the child expects may happen on the ride home and whether the accompanying parent has in any way scripted, coached, bribed or threatened the child (Garber, 2014).

With these and related proximal pressures in mind, it is often wise to complete this interview procedure twice with the child on separate occasions, once when delivered by dad and once when delivered by mom.

By way of rationale I recommend playing dumb:

"I'm really sorry. I know that we did something like this the other day, but I have so many papers. Could you help me with this just one more time?"

Perceptions of My Child
© 2015 Benjamin D. Garber, Ph.D.

A separate copy of this questionnaire must be completed regarding each child.

Please print your name: _____

Please print your role in this child's life
(e.g., father, nanny, babysitter, teacher) _____

Please print the child's name: _____

Please print the child's date of birth: _____   Today's date: _____

This questionnaire is intended to help you to describe a particular child. For each of the following numbered items, please circle one number indicating how you see this child. For example,

Example: THIS CHILD IS POLITE

Never	1	2	3	4	5	6	7	8	9	10	Always

Where 1= never polite ... 5=sometimes polite ... and 10=always polite
The checkmark in box "7" indicates that this child is seen as often but not always polite.

Please take the time to answer each item accurately. Please keep in mind that there is no correct answer except what you see about your child. Please mark ONE NUMBER only for each item.

1. THIS CHILD MAKES FRIENDS EASILY

Never	1	2	3	4	5	6	7	8	9	10	Always

2. THIS CHILD DOES AS I SAY

Never	1	2	3	4	5	6	7	8	9	10	Always

3. THIS CHILD HAS TROUBLE FALLING ASLEEP

Never	1	2	3	4	5	6	7	8	9	10	Always

4. THIS CHILD HAS A HEALTHY DIET

Never	1	2	3	4	5	6	7	8	9	10	Always

5. THIS CHILD IS SCARED

Never	1	2	3	4	5	6	7	8	9	10	Always

Likert (continuum) Ratings are familiar to many adults.

These items often elicit in-between and extreme responses. The nature of this instrument does not require precision.

Hypothesis building:

Is the child experiencing significant emotional distress?

1. Friends easily (low)
3. Trouble sleeping (high)
5. Scared (high)
9. Angry (high)
11. Worried (high)
14. Wets the bed (high)*
18. Clingy (high)*
23. Resists change (high)
27. Secretive (high)
28. Sad (high)
36. Overeats (high)
37. Prefers younger (high)
43. Bad habits (high)

Nothing is ever simple:
All responses must be understood in context.
Items marked with an asterisk may be particularly sensitive to development/age, trauma history and/or health considerations.

Perceptions of My Child

Child's Name: _____ Your Name: _____   page 2 of 5

6. THIS CHILD ONLY TELLS THE TRUTH

| Never | 1 | 2 | 3 | 4 | 5 | 6 | 7 | 8 | 9 | 10 | Always |

7. THIS CHILD KNOWS WHAT THE RULES AND EXPECTATIONS ARE IN THIS HOME

| Never | 1 | 2 | 3 | 4 | 5 | 6 | 7 | 8 | 9 | 10 | Always |

8. THIS CHILD IS SUCCESSFUL AT SCHOOL

| Never | 1 | 2 | 3 | 4 | 5 | 6 | 7 | 8 | 9 | 10 | Always |

9. THIS CHILD IS ANGRY

| Never | 1 | 2 | 3 | 4 | 5 | 6 | 7 | 8 | 9 | 10 | Always |

10. THIS CHILD DOES HIS OR HER CHORES

| Never | 1 | 2 | 3 | 4 | 5 | 6 | 7 | 8 | 9 | 10 | Always |

11. THIS CHILD IS A WORRIER

| Never | 1 | 2 | 3 | 4 | 5 | 6 | 7 | 8 | 9 | 10 | Always |

12. THIS CHILD PREFERS TO BE WITH ADULTS

| Never | 1 | 2 | 3 | 4 | 5 | 6 | 7 | 8 | 9 | 10 | Always |

13. THIS CHILD IS HAPPY

| Never | 1 | 2 | 3 | 4 | 5 | 6 | 7 | 8 | 9 | 10 | Always |

14. THIS CHILD WETS THE BED

| Never | 1 | 2 | 3 | 4 | 5 | 6 | 7 | 8 | 9 | 10 | Always |

15. AFTER WE'VE BEEN APART, THIS CHILD IS HAPPY TO SEE ME

| Never | 1 | 2 | 3 | 4 | 5 | 6 | 7 | 8 | 9 | 10 | Always |

Hypothesis building:

Is the child triangulated into the adult conflict and/or enmeshed with the respondent?

12. Prefers to be with adults (high)

15. Happy to see me (high)*

16. Asks me advice (high)

27. Secretive (high)

30. Loves other parent (low)

31. Needs me (high)

33. Get away from me (high)

34. Reminds me of myself (high)

35. Understands me (high)

40. Enrages me (high)

44. Helps me (high)

Hypothesis building?

With the benefit of an adequate and representative data set, responses to this questionnaire might be factor analyzed so as to generate statistically reliable and meaningful interpretive categories. In the absence of those data, I offer here clues that might inform hypotheses relevant to family dynamics.

Forensic family evaluation is, after all, about generating well-informed guesses (hypotheses) and then proceeding to discover which data confirm and which disconfirm so as to arrive at conclusions and recommendations.

FORM 10: Perceptions of My Child

Page 3 of 5

Perceptions of My Child

Child's Name: _____ Your Name: _____   page 3 of 5

16. THIS CHILD ASKS ME ADVICE
Never | 1 | 2 | 3 | 4 | 5 | 6 | 7 | 8 | 9 | 10 | Always

17. THIS CHILD IS WELL COORDINATED
Never | 1 | 2 | 3 | 4 | 5 | 6 | 7 | 8 | 9 | 10 | Always

18. THIS CHILD CLINGS TO ME
Never | 1 | 2 | 3 | 4 | 5 | 6 | 7 | 8 | 9 | 10 | Always

19. THIS CHILD NEEDS PREDICTABILITY AND ROUTINE
Never | 1 | 2 | 3 | 4 | 5 | 6 | 7 | 8 | 9 | 10 | Always

20. THIS CHILD STEALS
Never | 1 | 2 | 3 | 4 | 5 | 6 | 7 | 8 | 9 | 10 | Always

21. THIS CHILD LIES
Never | 1 | 2 | 3 | 4 | 5 | 6 | 7 | 8 | 9 | 10 | Always

22. THIS CHILD IS LOVING AND AFFECTIONATE
Never | 1 | 2 | 3 | 4 | 5 | 6 | 7 | 8 | 9 | 10 | Always

23. THIS CHILD RESISTS CHANGE
Never | 1 | 2 | 3 | 4 | 5 | 6 | 7 | 8 | 9 | 10 | Always

24. THIS CHILD IS OVER-ACTIVE
Never | 1 | 2 | 3 | 4 | 5 | 6 | 7 | 8 | 9 | 10 | Always

25. THIS CHILD LIKES HIM- OR HERSELF
Never | 1 | 2 | 3 | 4 | 5 | 6 | 7 | 8 | 9 | 10 | Always

26. THIS CHILD IS ARTISTIC
Never | 1 | 2 | 3 | 4 | 5 | 6 | 7 | 8 | 9 | 10 | Always

Hypothesis building:

Is the child emotionally resilient, mature and/or responsible?

2. Makes friends easily (high)

3. Trouble falling asleep (low)

4. Healthy diet (high)

8. Successful at school (high)*

13. Happy (high)

14. Wets the bed (never)

17. Well-coordinated (high)

23. Resists change (low)

25. Likes self (high)

26. Artistic (high)

32. Patient (high)

39. Healthy (high)

42. Funny (high)

45. Needy (low)

---

23. This child resists change.

Inquire further: Managing transition, novelty and spontaneity is harder for some people than others. Individuals with autism spectrum difficulties or attachment disorders may find change very hard routinely.

When stress increases, the individual's capacity to manage change can diminish sharply. A parent's high response to this item can easily confound personality predisposition with reaction to acute circumstances.

FORM 10: Perceptions of My Child
Page 4 of 5

Perceptions of My Child

Child's Name: _____ Your Name: _____   page 4 of 5

27. THIS CHILD IS SECRETIVE .

| Never | 1 | 2 | 3 | 4 | 5 | 6 | 7 | 8 | 9 | 10 | Always |

28. THIS CHILD IS SAD .

| Never | 1 | 2 | 3 | 4 | 5 | 6 | 7 | 8 | 9 | 10 | Always |

29. THIS CHILD WATCHES TELEVISION .

| Never | 1 | 2 | 3 | 4 | 5 | 6 | 7 | 8 | 9 | 10 | Always |

30. THIS CHILD LOVES HIS OR HER OTHER PARENT .

| Never | 1 | 2 | 3 | 4 | 5 | 6 | 7 | 8 | 9 | 10 | Always |

31. THIS CHILD NEEDS ME .

| Never | 1 | 2 | 3 | 4 | 5 | 6 | 7 | 8 | 9 | 10 | Always |

32. THIS CHILD IS PATIENT .

| Never | 1 | 2 | 3 | 4 | 5 | 6 | 7 | 8 | 9 | 10 | Always |

33. THIS CHILD WANTS TO GET AWAY FROM ME .

| Never | 1 | 2 | 3 | 4 | 5 | 6 | 7 | 8 | 9 | 10 | Always |

34. THIS CHILD REMINDS ME OF MYSELF WHEN I WAS A CHILD .

| Never | 1 | 2 | 3 | 4 | 5 | 6 | 7 | 8 | 9 | 10 | Always |

35. THIS CHILD UNDERSTANDS ME .

| Never | 1 | 2 | 3 | 4 | 5 | 6 | 7 | 8 | 9 | 10 | Always |

36. THIS CHILD OVEREATS .

| Never | 1 | 2 | 3 | 4 | 5 | 6 | 7 | 8 | 9 | 10 | Always |

---

30. This child loves his or her other parent.

Inquire further: Why or why not? Does the respondent support this opportunity in word and in deed?

---

33. This child wants to get away from me.

Inquire further: Children need to grow away from caregivers and toward independence. What does this response say about the parent-child relationship?

A parent who resents healthy separation may be infantilizing.

---

35. This child understands me.

Inquire further: The focus should be on the adult understanding the child.

Does a high response here suggests that the adult is getting his or her needs met from the child (i.e., adultification; e.g., Wells et al., 1999)?

The risk of parentification is exacerbated when parents separate and divorce (e.g., Jurkovic et al., 2001; Peris et al., 2008).

FORM 10:
Perceptions of My Child
Page 5 of 5

Perceptions of My Child

Child's Name: _____ Your Name: _____   page 5 of 5

37. THIS CHILD PREFERS TO PLAY WITH YOUNGER CHILDREN

| Never | 1 | 2 | 3 | 4 | 5 | 6 | 7 | 8 | 9 | 10 | Always |

38. THIS CHILD IS GOOD LOOKING

| Never | 1 | 2 | 3 | 4 | 5 | 6 | 7 | 8 | 9 | 10 | Always |

39. THIS CHILD IS HEALTHY

| Never | 1 | 2 | 3 | 4 | 5 | 6 | 7 | 8 | 9 | 10 | Always |

40. THIS CHILD ENRAGES ME

| Never | 1 | 2 | 3 | 4 | 5 | 6 | 7 | 8 | 9 | 10 | Always |

41. THIS CHILD IS SAFE

| Never | 1 | 2 | 3 | 4 | 5 | 6 | 7 | 8 | 9 | 10 | Always |

42. THIS CHILD IS FUNNY

| Never | 1 | 2 | 3 | 4 | 5 | 6 | 7 | 8 | 9 | 10 | Always |

43. THIS CHILD HAS BAD HABITS

| Never | 1 | 2 | 3 | 4 | 5 | 6 | 7 | 8 | 9 | 10 | Always |

44. THIS CHILD HELPS ME WITH MY PROBLEMS

| Never | 1 | 2 | 3 | 4 | 5 | 6 | 7 | 8 | 9 | 10 | Always |

45. THIS CHILD IS NEEDY

| Never | 1 | 2 | 3 | 4 | 5 | 6 | 7 | 8 | 9 | 10 | Always |

46. THIS CHILD IS AGGRESSIVE

| Never | 1 | 2 | 3 | 4 | 5 | 6 | 7 | 8 | 9 | 10 | Always |

40. This child enrages me.

Inquire further: "Enrages" suggests an extreme loss of perspective, roles and boundaries. Does this suggest possible violence? Is this perhaps the respondent's projection of feelings about the other parent on the child?

41. This child is safe.

A low response calls for immediate inquiry:

Revelation of a threat to the child's safety may trigger mandated reporting obligations.

44. This child helps me with my problems.

Inquire further: Once again, a high response flags concerns with boundaries and alignment. Is this an enmeshed (e.g., adultified or Parentified) dyad (e.g., Garber, 2011).

Beware that gender (e.g., Mayseless & Scharf, 2009; Katz et al., 2009), culture (e.g., Oznobishin, & Kurman, 2009), poverty (Burton, 2007; MacMahon & Luthar, 2007) and birth order are relevant (e.g., Manzi et al., 2006; Walsh et al., 2006).

Caretaker health may be also relevant (e.g., Thomkins, 2007; Stein et al., 2007).

Perceptions of My Child Summary Sheet
(scoring and interpretation)

Perceptions of My Child 2006
© 2015 Benjamin D. Garber, Ph.D.
Summary Sheet

Item	Parent A 1-10	Parent B 1-10	DIFF SCORE	>3?
1. This child makes friends easily				
2. This child does as I say				
3. This child has trouble falling asleep				
4. This child has a healthy diet				
5. This child is scared				
6. This child only tells the truth				
7. This child knows what the rules and expectations are in this home				
8. This child is successful at school				
9. This child is angry				
10. This child does his or her chores				
11. This child is a worrier				
12. This child prefers to be with adults				
13. This child is happy				
14. This child wets the bed				
15. After we've been apart, This child is happy to see me				
16. This child asks me advice				
17. This child is well coordinated				
18. This child clings to me				
19. This child needs predictability and routine				
20. This child steals				
21. This child lies				
22. This child is loving and affectionate				
23. This child resists change				
24. This child is overactive				
25. This child likes him- or herself				
26. This child is artistic				
27. This child is secretive				
28. This child is sad				
29. This child watches television				
30. This child loves his or her other parent				
31. This child needs me				
32. This child is patient				
33. This child wants to get away from me				
34. This child reminds me of myself when I was a child				
35. This child understands me				
36. This child overeats				
37. This child prefers to play with younger children				
38. This child is good looking				
39. This child is healthy				
40. This child enrages me				
41. This child is safe				
42. This child is funny				
43. This child has bad habits				
44. This child helps me with my problems				
45. This child is needy				
46. This child is aggressive				

First:

Record Parent A's numeric (0-10) responses down this column in sequential order.

Second:

Records Parent B's numeric (0-10) responses down the adjoining column in sequential order.

Third:

Subtract across rows to find the absolute difference score.

Example:

Parent A's response = 9

Parent B's response = 5

Difference score = 4

Fourth:

An absolute difference of greater than or equal to three between Parent A and Parent B is noted in the far right column.

Three is an arbitrary landmark. In general, the bigger the difference between caregivers' ratings, the more valuable further inquiry.

References

Burton, L. (2007). Childhood adultification in economically disadvantaged families: A conceptual model. Family Relations, 56, 329–345.

Garber, Benjamin D. (2011). Parental alienation and the dynamics of the enmeshed dyad: Adultification, parentification and infantilization. *Family Court Review*, 49(2), 322-335.

Jurkovic, G. J., Thirkield, A., & Morrell, R. (2001). Parentification of adult children of divorce: A multidimensional analysis. *Journal of Youth and Adolescence*, 30, 245–257.

Katz, J., Petracca, M., & Rabinowitz, J. (2009). A retrospective study of daughters' emotional role reversal with parents, attachment anxiety, excessive reassurance-seeking, and depressive symptoms. *The American Journal of Family Therapy*, 37, 185–195.

Manzi, C., Vignoles, V. L., Regalia, C., & Scabini, E. (2006). Cohesion and enmeshment revisited: Differentiation, identity, and well-being in two European cultures. *Journal of Marriage and Family*, 68, 673–689.

Mayseless, O., & Scharf, M. (2009). Too close for comfort: Inadequate boundaries with parents and individuation in late adolescent girls. *American Journal of Orthopsychiatry*, 79, 191–202.

McMahon, T. J., & Luthar, S. S. (2007). Defining characteristics and potential consequences of caretaking burden among children living in poverty. *American Journal of Orthopsychiatry*, 77, 267–281.

Oznobishin, O., & Kurman, J. (2009). Parent–child role reversal and psychological adjustment among immigrant youth in Israel. *Journal of Family Psychology*, 23, 405–415.

Peris, T. S., Goeke-Morey, M. C., Cummings, E. M., & Emery, R. E. (2008). Marital conflict and support seeking by parents in adolescence: Empirical support for the parentification construct. *Journal of Family Psychology*, 22, 633–642.

Stein, J., Rotheram-Borus, M. J., & Lester, P. (2007). Impact of parentification on long-term outcomes among children of parents with HIV/AIDS. *Family Process*, 46, 317–333.

Tompkins, T. L. (2007). Parentification and maternal HIV infection: Beneficial role or pathological burden? *Journal of Child and Family Studies*, 16, 113–125.

Walsh, S., Shulman, S., Bar-On, Z., & Tsur, A. (2006). The role of parentification and family climate in adaptation among immigrant adolescents in Israel. *Journal of Research on Adolescence*, 16, 321–350.

Wells, M., Glickauf-Hughes, C., & Jones, R. (1999). Co-dependency: A grass roots construct's relationship to shame-proneness, low self-esteem, and childhood parentification. *American Journal of Family Therapy*, 27, 63–71.

G. Index of Terms and Concepts

About Benjamin D. Garber, PhD

I am a New Hampshire licensed psychologist, parenting coordinator and former Guardian ad litem. My work is divided among clinical services to children and families, evaluative services for the courts and expert consultation services in family law matters. I frequently have the privilege of addressing audiences eager to improve their skills understanding and serving the needs of children across the English-speaking world. I also write compulsively both for the popular press and professional publications in psychology and the law. Across these and related roles, my singular commitment is to the well-being of children.

This volume is dedicated to Laura, Mollie and Zoe who give meaning to every day.

I am grateful to and awestruck by Megan Hunter, entrepreneur, and the motivating force that brings this publication and all of her excellent Unhooked Media productions to life.

Dr. Garber's website is: www.healthyparent.com.

Other Books by Dr. Garber

A Roadmap to the Parenting Plan Worksheet (2015)

The Healthy Parent's ABC's (2015)

Letting Go—Holding Tight: Raising Healthy Kids in Troubled Times (coming 2016)

Developmental Psychology for Family Law Professionals: Theory, Application and the Best Interests of the Child (2009)

Keeping Kids Out of the Middle: Child-Centered Parenting in the Midst of Conflict, Separation, and Divorce (2008)

All are available at www.UnhookedBooks.com

www.ingramcontent.com/pod-product-compliance
Lightning Source LLC
Chambersburg PA
CBHW080555270326
41929CB00019B/3325